SELECTED WORKS OF
JOSÉ CARLOS MARIÁTEGUI

SELECTED WORKS

OF

JOSÉ CARLOS MARIÁTEGUI

Edited and Translated
by Christian Noakes

ISKRA
BOOKS

This edition published by Iskra Books 2021

Based on original translations of various selections from José Mariátegui: from the lectures and essays, "The World Crisis and the Peruvian Proletariat," "Marxist Determination," "The Problem of the Indian," "The Problem of Race in Latin America," "Programmatic Principles of the Socialist Party," "Anti-Imperialist Point of View," "Nationalism and Vanguardism," "Heterodoxy of Tradition," "The Freedom of Education," and "Pessimism of Reality, Optimism of the Ideal." First published in Spanish

Iskra Books
US | UK | Ireland | Canada | Australia | Brazil | South Africa
www.communiststudies.org

Iskra Books is the imprint of the *Center for Communist Studies*, an international research center dedicated to the advancement of academic and public scholarship in the field of Marxist-Leninist studies.

ISBN-13: 978-1-0879-4300-8

British Library Cataloguing in Publication Data
A catalogue record for this book is available from the British Library

Library of Congress Cataloging-in-Publication Data
A catalog record for this book is available from the Library of Congress

Typeset by Ben Stahnke
Map by Lydia Kurtz
Printed and Distributed by IngramSpark

CONTENTS

For the Aymara and the Quechua peoples.

*"Here we are, the sons of Bolivar, the sons of Guaicaipuru,
the sons of Túpac Amaru! And we are determined to be free!"*

-Hugo Chávez

PRIMARY GEOGRAPHIC REGIONS OF PERU

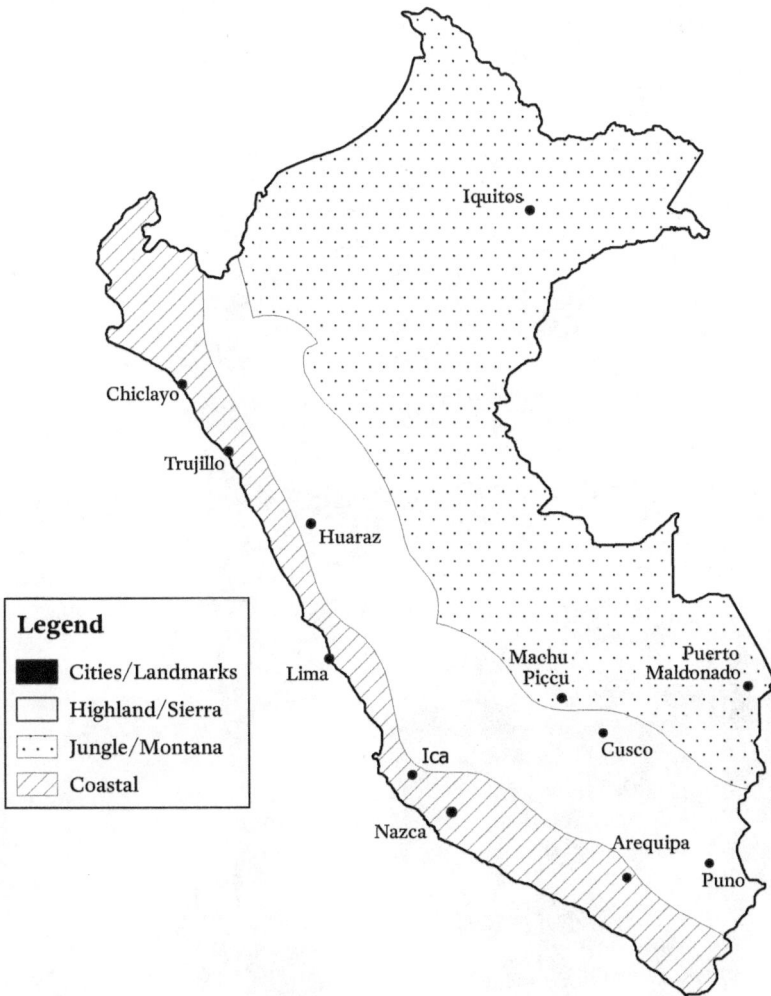

Legend
- ■ Cities/Landmarks
- ☐ Highland/Sierra
- ⠂ Jungle/Montana
- ▨ Coastal

Iquitos

Chiclayo

Trujillo

Huaraz

Lima

Machu Picchu

Puerto Maldonado

Cusco

Ica

Nazca

Arequipa

Puno

INTRODUCTION

José Carlos Mariátegui was born in Moquegua, Peru, to a poor *mestizo* family on July 14, 1894. Considered by many to be the father of Latin American Communism, he is celebrated for being the first person to utilize Marxist methods of analysis in order to better understand concrete reality in Peru and for carving a path to revolution based off of these particular historical conditions. As such, he was one of the first Latin American socialists to acknowledge the revolutionary potential of the peasantry and Indigenous peoples. Rather than take a paternalistic or humanitarian position, Mariátegui believed that these overlapping groups needed to be the architects of their own liberation and to do so using their own cultural knowledge, experience, and language.[1] The attention he paid to these marginalized populations in both his thought and organizing efforts set him apart from many of his contemporaries, providing an ideological foundation for the melding of revolutionary socialism and *Indigenismo* throughout the region.

Due to financial hardship, Mariátegui left school

after the eighth grade in order to provide additional income for his family. When he was fifteen, he began work as a copy boy for the newspaper *La Prensa*. Displaying remarkable talent and dedication, he quickly rose to editing and writing positions. After working as an editor and contributor for several publications, he co-founded the socialist newspaper *La Razón* with César Falcón in 1919. While far from the revolutionary publications of his later years, this newspaper represented an important development in Mariátegui's political consciousness. The paper threw its vocal and uncompromising support behind a wave of worker militancy, which developed out of increased agitation for an eight-hour work day, and the university reform movement that began in Argentina before spreading to other Latin American nations.[2]

In response to the pro-worker and student positions, as well as opposition to the Peruvian government, put forward in *La Razón*, the dictator Augusto B. Leguía effectively exiled Mariátegui and Falcón to Europe in 1919, where they immersed themselves in the socialist and intellectual currents of Europe and began conceptualizing what the road to socialism would look like in Peru. Mariátegui's journey began in France where he met Henri Barbusse, Romain Rolland, and other communist intellectuals. While Mariátegui's stay in France helped further develop his political consciousness, the most revolutionary transformation of this period occurred during the three years he spent in Italy at a time when the country was submersed in both revolutionary and reactionary fervor. During this essential portion of his journey through Europe he witnessed the creation of the

Communist Party of Italy (CPI) and came into contact with leading revolutionary intellectuals—such as Antonio Gramsci. It was in Italy that he became an avowed Marxist-Leninist committed to the international communist movement.[3]

Upon returning to Peru in 1923, he began giving lectures to workers and students at the González Prada Popular University. In these lectures, he "stressed that the workers should seek to understand world issues from the point of view of their own class interests and culture" and he encouraged "workers to feel that they were more than merely spectators of the world crisis, but were actively and inextricably involved."[4] His conception of a popular education, in many ways, prefigured the pedagogical model of the Brazilian Paulo Freire. In contrast to the dominant system that reinforced oppressive social relations, Mariátegui promoted popular education as a means of developing the class consciousness of the oppressed masses, which he saw as a necessity for successful revolution. He believed that Marxism-Leninism in particular would "open the shining path to revolution."

Mariátegui founded the journal *Amauta* (Queche term meaning "wise one" or "teacher"), his most ambitious and groundbreaking publication, in 1926. For the journal's four years of circulation, it brought forward a vanguardist vision that melded the political and artistic worlds through its publication of political prose, fiction, poetry, and visual arts. While contributors did not always share a common political tendency, "the goal *Amauta* set for itself was nothing less than to create a polarization of intellectuals along political lines in Peru; and, then to bring about a concentration of followers behind the ideological banner of revolution and socialism."[5] The publication was largely successful in drawing both readers and contributors toward these ends and exposed many to both *Indigenismo* and Marxism-Leninism.[6]

Alongside *Amauta,* Mariátegui founded the newspaper *Labor.* This paper was highly successful in reaching Peru's working class and instilling in them a revolutionary class consciousness.[7] Released roughly every two weeks, it featured articles ranging from proletarian art, literature, politics, economics, worker and Indigenous organizing, and campaigns against unsafe or exploitative working conditions.[8] Taken together, *Amauta* and *Labor* were monumental endeavors that served to blur the lines between workers and intellectuals and promote a revolutionary worker-peasant alliance.

But he was not simply a prolific writer. According to Peruvian communist Jorge del Prado:

Mariátegui was ... the first in Peru to dispense with mere metaphysical and sentimental declarations about the situation of the working class, the first to seriously care about indigenous and peasant women, the first to replace the work of "school teachers" and wet nurses who insist on playing ... with combative acts of organizing, with the active and constant struggle for their immediate and long-term needs. As in Lenin's work, Mariátegui's theoretical solutions to the specific problems of our social reality always have a marked practical sense.[9]

The practical or material grounding of his theories was, by itself, a monumental contribution to the struggle of oppressed and exploited Peruvians. However, his revolutionary activities went well beyond the written word. In 1928, he founded the Peruvian Socialist Party—a Marxist-Leninist vanguard party that sought to unite the country's urban and rural working class under the direction of a core group of communists and connect the national struggle to the internationalist communist movement via the Third International. As the party's first secretary-general, he developed party cadre from working-class and Indigenous populations who then organized their communities.[10] Among the party's activities was the creation of the General Confederation of Peruvian Workers (CGTP)—a Marxist trade union federation that worked in tandem with the party to organize and unite the urban and rural masses.[11]

Mariátegui is celebrated for utilizing Marxism to understand, and thus transform, the concrete conditions of Peruvian society. As such, he is often portrayed as representing an antagonistic alternative to the politics of the Third International—a political body that he was in fact highly supportive of and affiliated with.[12] Rather than put him at odds with other communist figures, his writings reflect the common and non-deterministic assertion that revolution is only successful when material conditions, which change in time and place, inform revolutionary practice. Lenin—who greatly influenced the Peruvian—was likewise aware of this necessity in building the Soviet revolution. It is worth noting that Lenin and the Bolsheviks were often denounced in their time for not following what economic determinists considered to be the universal instructions for all socialist revolutions and instead actively built a revolution through constant consideration of their particular circumstances. In Mariátegui's own words "Marxism, where it has shown itself to be revolutionary—that is, where it has been Marxist—has never obeyed a passive and rigid determinism."[13] He saw himself as belonging to the heterogenous and dynamic "tradition" of communist thought. In line with Lenin and the development of Marxism-Leninism, Mariátegui offered a thorough historical materialist analysis that situated the local or particular within a larger understanding of the Marxist method and the international struggle for socialism in the age of imperialism. He fully understood that Marxism is not a static or rigid set of instructions but a means of understanding the particular—which is intimately linked to the global struggle—in order to determine the means of revolution. The uniqueness that comes from a localized strategy is not in contradiction with communist revolution but a prerequisite for it.

Mariátegui's emphasis on the revolutionary role of peasant and Indigenous masses, the subjective factor of class consciousness, and the dialectical relationship between nationalism and internationalism have had a lasting impact on both Peruvian Marxism and Latin American Marxism as a whole. His influence on revolutionaries in Nicaragua and Cuba has been particularly pronounced.[14] Founding members of the Sandinista National Liberation Front (FSLN), Carlos Fonseca and Tomás Borge, drew heavily from Mariátegui for their own strategy to liberate Nicaragua

from the oppression of US imperialism and their com-
prador lackeys. His influence is particularly apparent
in the Sandinista's focus on rural communities and
their explicitly socialist and internationalist manifestation of revolutionary nationalism. In Cuba, his writings informed communist thought both prior to and
after the 1959 revolution. Already widely read in the
island's socialist circles, Fidel Castro encountered the
Peruvian's works while in prison from 1953 to 1955.[15]
During his expedition around South America in 1952,
Ernesto "Che" Guevara was introduced to Mariátegui's thought by Hugo Pesce—a Peruvian doctor
who had been in the secret communist cell that directed the Peruvian Socialist Party along with Mariátegui.
Pesce also co-authored pieces with Mariátegui and
served as a representative for him abroad.[16] Mariátegui would come to have a lasting impact on Guevara's political consciousness. The former believed
that "the proletariat must elevate itself to a 'produc-
er's morality', quite distant and distinct from the
'slave morality.'"[17] Successful revolutions require a
radical shift in the way people conceive of and interact
with the world around them. Guided by revolutionary
class consciousness, people can thus contribute to the
daily tasks of building a socialist society. This informed Guevara's own belief that "to build communism it is necessary, simultaneous with the new material foundations, to build the new man and woman."[18]
After the success of the Cuban revolution, Guevara
was the leading proponent of publishing Mariátegui's
work.[19] The latter's writings on revolutionary myths
and socialist ethics also informed the conception of
liberation theology. This foundational influence is evident in the works of the Peruvian priest and philoso-

pher Gustavo Gutiérrez.[20] Unlike many in the Church who have historically exploited, oppressed, and slaughtered under the pretext of their religion, Gutiérrez saw Marxist class struggle as a means of realizing Christian teachings in practice. Mariátegui's work was no doubt a central component in the melding of Marxism and Christian social teachings throughout Latin America—a relationship that is in many ways unique to the region.

The following collection of Mariátegui's writings has been published for three interrelated reasons. First, his contributions to Marxist thought are little known in much of the English-speaking world—an error we hope to play a part in correcting. Second, he is often misrepresented by non-communists who paint him as a reformist or non-communist in direct contrast to his unyielding commitment to Leninist revolution. This tendency is common among petit-bourgeois academics and social democrats. As Lenin puts it, "attempts are made to turn them [revolutionaries] into harmless icons... while at the same emasculating and vulgarizing the real essence of their revolutionary theories and blunting their revolutionary edge."[21] Whether an intentional distortion or an honest misconception, such domestication serves the interests of counter-revolutionaries. Lastly, his writings remain relevant to contemporary struggles against capitalism and imperialism and can therefore contribute greatly to revolutionary praxis. His writing refutes what is all too common in the left of the global North—reformism, the influence of imperialist ideology, and bourgeois idealism.

To aid in translating these works, I have consulted

the invaluable collection compiled by Harry E. Vanden and Marc Becker.[22] I have also consulted Majory Urquidi's translation of "The Problem of the Indian."[23] I would also like to thank Antony LeRoy for their help in translating the present volume.

Christian Noakes

The Center for Communist Studies

1

THE WORLD CRISIS AND THE PERUVIAN PROLETARIAT

June 15, 1923 Lecture at
González Prada Popular University

In this conference—let's call it a conversation rather than a conference—I will limit myself to explaining the subject matter of the course, while at the same time providing some considerations on the necessity of knowledge of the world crisis among the proletariat.

Unfortunately, Peru lacks an educational press that follows the development of this great crisis with intelligence and ideological conviction. There is also a lack of university professors like José Ingenieros[1] who are capable of becoming passionate about renovative ideas that are currently transforming the world and liberating it from the influence and prejudices of conservative bourgeois culture and education. Also lacking are socialist and unionist groups in possession of their own instruments of popular culture, and thus capable of making people interested in studying the crisis. The only course of popular education with a revolutionary spirit is this one, developed at the Popular University. It thus falls to it, beyond its modest initial plan, to present contemporary reality to the people, to explain to the people that they are living in one of the most momentous and greatest hours in history, to infect the people with the fruitful restlessness that it is currently stirring up other civilized peoples of the world.

In this great contemporary crisis the proletariat is not a spectator; it is an actor. The fate of the world proletariat will be resolved within it. Out of it will emerge, according to all probabilities and according to all forecasts, the proletarian civilization, the socialist civilization, destined to succeed the decadent, moribund, and individualist bourgeois society. Now, more than ever, the proletariat needs to know what is happening in the world. It cannot know it through the fragmentary, episodic, and homeopathic reports of the daily cable—in most cases, badly translated and worse written—coming always from reactionary agencies in charge of discrediting revolutionary parties, organizations, and men, thereby discouraging and disorientating the world proletariat.

In the European crisis, the destinies of all workers in the world are at stake. The development of the crisis must therefore interest the workers of Peru as well as the workers of the Far East. The crisis has Europe as its main stage; but the crisis of European institutions is the crisis of the institutions of Western civilization. And Peru, like the other countries in the Americas, rotates within the orbit of this civilization, not only because they are politically independent but economically colonial countries linked to the chariots of British, U.S., or French capitalism, but because our cultural institutions are European. And it is precisely these democratic institutions and culture, which we copy from Europe, that are now in a definitive period of total crisis in Europe. Above all, capitalist civilization has internationalized the life of humanity; it has created material ties between all peoples that establish among them an inevitable solidarity. Internationalism is not just an ideal; it is a historical reality. Progress makes the interests, ideas, customs, and regimes of the peoples unify and comingle. Peruvians, like the other American peoples, are therefore not outside the crisis; they are within it. The global crisis has already had an impact on these peoples. And, of course, it will continue to have an impact. A period of reaction in Europe will also be a period of reaction in America. A period of revolution in Europe will also be a period of revolution in America. More than a century ago, when the life of humanity was not as interlinked as it is today, when today's media did not exist, when nations did not have the immediate and constant contact that they have today, when there was no press, when we were still distant spectators of European events, the French Revolution gave rise to the War of Independence and the emergence of all these republics. This memory is enough for us to realize how quickly the transformation of society will be reflected in American societies. Those who say that Peru, and America in general, live far removed from the European revolution, have no notion of contemporary life, nor do they even have an approximate understanding of history. These people are surprised that Europe's most advanced ideals reach Peru. But, by contrast, they are not surprised that the airplane, the ocean liner, the wireless telegraph, or the radio arrive. These are all, in short, the most advanced expressions of Europe's material progress. There would be the same reason for ignoring the socialist movement as there would be for ignoring Einstein's theory of relativity. I am sure that the most reactionary of our intellectuals—almost all of them are impenetrably reactionary—would not think that the new physics of Einstein should be banned from study and dissemination.

The proletariat, in general, needs to learn about the great dimensions of the world crisis. This need is even greater in socialist, laborite, syndicalist, or libertarian segments of the proletariat which constitute its vanguard. It is greater in that part of the proletariat that is more combative, conscious, and prepared. It is greater in those parts of the proletariat in charge of directing the great proletarian actions, and it is greater in that part of the proletariat that has the historical role of representing the Peruvian proletariat in the present social moment. It is greatest in that part of the proletariat, whatever its particular creed, that has a revolutionary class consciousness.

Above all, I dedicate my lectures to this vanguard of the Peruvian proletariat. No one needs to study the world crisis more than vanguard proletarians. I do not intend to come to this free platform of a free university to teach you the history of this world crisis, but to study it with you. Comrades, I do not teach you the history of this world crisis from this podium; I study it with you. In this study, I have only the very modest merit of contributing the personal observations of three and a half years of European life—that is, of the three and a half years culminating in the crisis—and the echoes of contemporary European thought.

For various reasons, I especially invite the vanguard of the proletariat to study the process of the world crisis with me. The first reason is that the revolutionary preparation, revolutionary culture, and revolutionary orientation of this proletarian vanguard has been formed on the basis of pre-war socialist, syndicalist, and anarchist literature—or at least literature predating the peak of the crisis. Generally, it is outdated socialist, syndicalist, and libertarian books that circulate among us. Here, a little is known of classic socialist and syndicalist literature. The new revolutionary literature is not known. Revolutionary culture here is a classical culture, in addition to being—as you all know, comrades—a very incipient, inorganic, disorderly, and incomplete culture. Now, all that pre-war socialist and syndicalist literature is under revision. And this revision is not a revision imposed by the whim of the theorists but by the force of events. This literature, therefore, cannot be used today without the benefit of an inventory. It, of course, has not ceased to be exact in its principles, in its foundations, in everything that is ideal and eternal in it; but it has often ceased to be exact in its tactical inspirations, in its historical considerations, in everything that signifies action, procedure, means of struggle. The goal of the workers remains the same; what has changed, as a necessary result of recent historical events, are the roads taken to arrive at (or even approach) that ideal goal. Hence, the study of these historical events, and their significance, is essential for militant working-class organizations.

You know, comrades, that the European proletarian forces are divided into two great camps: reformists and revolutionaries. There is a reformist, collaborationist, evolutionist Workers International and another maximalist, anti-collaborationist, revolutionary Workers International. Between one and the other, an intermediate International has tried to emerge. But that has concluded by making common cause with the first against the second. There are nuances on both sides; but there are clearly and unmistakably only two: the camp of those who want to achieve socialism by collaborating politically with the bourgeoisie; and the camp of those who want to achieve socialism by fully seizing political power for the proletariat. And good, the existence of these two sides comes from the existence of two different conceptions, from two opposite conceptions, from two antithetical conceptions of the current historical moment. A part of the proletariat believes that the moment is not revolutionary; that the bourgeoisie has not yet exhausted its historical function; that, on the contrary, the bourgeoisie is still strong enough to retain political power; that the hour of social revolution has not arrived. The other part of the proletariat believes that the current historical moment is revolutionary; that the bourgeoisie is incapable of rebuilding the social wealth destroyed by war and incapable, therefore, of solving the problems of peace; that the war has created a crisis whose solution can only be a proletarian solution, a socialist solution; and that with the Russian Revolution the social revolution has begun.

There are, then, two proletarian armies because

there are in the proletariat two opposite conceptions of the historical moment, two different interpretations of the world crisis. The numerical strength of one or the other proletarian armies depends on whether or not events appear to confirm their respective historical conception. Because of this, the thinkers, theorists, and scholars of one or the other proletarian armies strive, above all, to delve deeply into the meaning of the crisis, to understand its character, to discover its significance.

Before the war, two tendencies divided the proletariat: the socialist tendency and the syndicalist tendency. The socialist tendency was predominantly reformist, social-democratic, and collaborationist. The socialists thought that the time for the social revolution was far off and they fought for gradual conquest through legal action and governmental or, at least, legislative collaboration. In some countries, this political action excessively weakened the revolutionary will and spirit of socialism. Socialism became considerably bourgeois. As a reaction against this turn, we had syndicalism. Syndicalism put forward the direct action of the unions in opposition to the political action of the socialist parties. The most revolutionary and intransigent spirits of the proletariat took refuge in syndicalism. But syndicalism also turned out to be somewhat collaborative and reformist in the end. It was was also dominated by a union bureaucracy without a true revolutionary mentality. Syndicalism and socialism also showed themselves to be more or less in solidarity and conjoined in some countries, such as Italy, where the Socialist Party did not participate in the government and remained faithful to other formal principles of independence. Such as it is, the tendencies—to some degree either at odds or unified, depending the country —were two: syndicalists and socialists. The revolutionary literature of this period of struggle is what has almost exclusively informed the mentality of our proetarian leaders.

But, after the war, the situation has changed. The proletarian camp, as we have just recalled, is no longer divided into socialists and syndicalists but into reformists and revolutionaries. First, we have witnessed a schism, a split in the socialist camp. One part of socialism has affirmed its social-democratic, collaborationist orientation; the other side has followed an anti-collaborationist, revolutionary orientation. And it is this part of socialism that, to clearly differentiate itself from the first, has adopted the name of communism. The division has also occurred in the same way in the union movement. One part of the unions support the social-democrats; the other part supports the communists. Consequently, the face of the European social struggle has radically changed. We have seen many intransigent pre-war trade unionists turn toward reformism, while we have seen others follow communism. And among latter, as Comrade Fonkén[2] has recently reminded us, is none other than the greatest and most illustrious theorist of syndicalism: the Frenchman Georges Sorel. Sorel—whose death has been a bitter mourning for the proletariat and intelligentsia of France—gave all his support to the Russian Revolution and to the men of the Russian Revolution.

Here, as in Europe, proletarians have to divide themselves not into syndicalists and socialists—an anachronistic classification—but into collaborationists and anti-collaborationists, reformists and revolutionaries. But for this classification to take place with clarity and coherence, it is essential that the proletariat know and understand the broad outlines of the great contemporary crisis. Confusion is inevitable if it is done any other way.

I share the opinion of those who believe that humanity is experiencing a revolutionary period. And I am convinced of the coming decline of all social-democratic theses, of all reformist theses, and of all incremental theses.

Before the war, these theses were understandable, because they corresponded to different historic conditions. Capitalism was at its peak. Production was overwhelming. Capitalism could afford the luxury of making successive economic concessions to the proletariat. And their profit margins were such that it was possible to form a large middle class, a large petite-bourgeoisie that enjoyed a convenient and comfortable sort of life. The European worker earned enough to eat, and in some nations, such as England and Germany, they were given sufficient resources to satisfy some spiritual needs. So there was no revolutionary atmosphere.

After the war, everything changed. Europe's social wealth was, to a large extent, destroyed. Capitalism, which was responsible for the war, now needs to rebuild that wealth at the expense of the proletariat. It, therefore, wants socialists to collaborate in the government, in order to strengthen its democratic institutions; but not to progress on the path to socialist fulfillment. Previously, the socialists collaborated to gradually improve the living conditions of the workers. Now

they collaborate to renounce all proletarian victory. To rebuild Europe, the bourgeoisie needs the proletariat to agree to produce more and consume less. The
proletariat resists one thing or another and tells itself
that it is not worth consolidating the power a social
class guilty of war and fatally destined to lead humanity to an even bloodier war. The conditions for the collaboration between the bourgeoisie and the proletariat
are, by nature, such that collaborationism must necessarily lose, little by little, its current widespread prose-
lytism.

Capitalism cannot make concessions to socialism. In order to rebuild, the European states need a
rigorous fiscal economy, an increase in working hours,
a decrease in wages, in a word, the reestablishment of
economic concepts and methods in opposition to proletarian desires. Logically, the proletariat cannot consent to this setback. Any possibility of rebuilding the
capitalist economy is thus eliminated. This is the
tragedy of contemporary Europe. In European countries, the reaction is revoking the economic concessions made to socialism. But, on one hand, this reactionary policy cannot be energetic or effective enough
to restore the bled-dry public treasury, and on the other hand, a united proletarian front against this reactionary policy is slowly developing. Fearful of revolution, the reaction therefore cancels not only the economic gains of the masses, but also threatens their political gains. We are thus witnessing the fascist dicta-
torship in Italy. But the bourgeoisie betrays and un-
dermines—and thus mortally wounds—democratic
institutions. And it loses all its moral force and ideological prestige.

Elsewhere, in the realm of international relations, the reaction puts foreign policy in the hands of the nationalist and anti-democratic minorities. And these nationalist minorities saturate that foreign policy with chauvinism. And, through their imperialist orientation and struggle for European hegemony, they prevent the reestablishment of an atmosphere of European solidarity, which would allow the countries to agree on a program of cooperation and work. We see the fruit of this nationalism, this reaction, in the occupation of the Ruhr.[3]

The world crisis is thus an economic crisis and a political crisis. And, above all, it is an ideological crisis. The affirmative, positivist philosophies of bourgeois society have long been undermined by a current of skepticism, of relativism. Rationalism, historicism, and positivism are declining irremediably. This is undoubtedly the most profound, most severe symptom of the crisis. This is the most definite and deepest indication that not only the economy of bourgeois society is in crisis, but that capitalist civilization, Western civilization, European civilization is in crisis as a whole.

Nevertheless, the ideologues of socialist revolution, Marx and Bakunin, Engels and Kropotkin, lived in the heyday of capitalist civilization and of historicist and positivist philosophy. Consequently, they could not foresee that the rise of the proletariat would have to take place by virtue of the decadence of Western civilization. The proletariat was destined to create a new type of civilization and culture. The economic ruin of the bourgeoisie was to be at the same time the ruin of the bourgeois civilization. And socialism was going to find that it had to govern not in a time of plenty, wealth, and abundance, but in a time of poverty, misery, and scarcity. Reformist socialists, accustomed to the idea that the socialist regime is more a regime of distribution than a regime of production, believe they see in this the symptom that the historical mission of the bourgeoisie is not yet finished and that the moment is not yet ripe to achieve socialism. In an article for *La Crónica*, I reported a phrases noting that the tragedy of Europe is this: capitalism can no longer and socialism cannot yet. This phrase, which does in fact give one a sense of the European tragedy, is the phrase of a reformist. It is a phrase saturated with an evolutionary mentality, and impregnated with the conception of a slow, gradual, and beatific pace, without convulsions and shock, from an individualist society to a collectivist society. And history teaches us that every new social state has been formed on the ruins of the preceding social state. And between the emergence of one and the collapse of the other there has been, logically, an intermediate period of crisis.

We are witnessing the disintegration, the agony of an outdated, senile, and decrepit society; and, at the same time, we are witnessing the gestation, the formation, the slow and restless elaboration of a new society. All the men who have a sincere ideological affiliation that ties us to this new society and separates us from the old society must fix our gaze deeply on this transcendental, agitated, and intense period of human history.

Source: *Historia de la Crisis Mundial*

2

MARXIST DETERMINISM

A frequent attitude of intellectuals who entertain themselves in denigrating the Marxist bibliography is to self-interestedly exaggerate the determinism of Marx and his school in order to declare them a product of the mechanistic mentality of the 19th century, incompatible with the heroic, voluntaristic conception of life to which the modern world is inclined since the end of the War. These reproaches do not accord with the criticism of the rationalist[1] and utopian superstitions and the mystical background of the socialist movement. But Henri de Man could not help but fall back on an argument that was so rampant among the intellectuals of the nineteenth century, seduced by the snobbery of the reaction against the "stupid nineteenth century." In this respect, the Belgian revisionist observes a certain prudence. "It must be stated," he declares, "that Marx does not deserve the reproach that is frequently aimed at him—that of being a fatalist, in the sense that he denies the influence of human will on historical development; what happens is that he considers this volition as predetermined."

He adds that "the disciples of Marx are right when they defend their teacher from the reproach of having preached that kind of fatalism." None of this, however, prevents him from accusing them of their "belief in another fatalism, that of inevitable categorical ends," since "according to the Marxist conception, there is a social will subject to laws, which is fulfilled through class struggle and the inevitable result of economic evolution that creates opposed interests."[2]

In substance, neo-revisionism adopts the idealist critique that reaffirms the action of the will and the spirit, although with discrete amendments. But this critique only pertains to the social-democratic orthodoxy which, as already established, is not and was not Marxist, but Lassallian—a fact proven by the vigor with which the slogan "back to Lassalle" is disseminated today inside German social democracy. For this criticism to be valid, one would have to start by proving that Marxism is social democracy, a work that Henri de Man avoids attempting. On the contrary, he recognizes the Third International as the heir to the International Association of Workers, in whose congress one can breathe a mysticism similar to that of the Christianity of the catacombs. And he states this explicit judgment:

> The vulgar Marxists of communism are the true beneficiaries of the Marxian heritage. They are not in the sense that they understand Marx better with reference to his era, but because they use him more effectively for the tasks of their era, to realize their objectives. Kautsky's image of Marx is more similar to the original than that which Lenin popularized among his disciples; but Kaut-

sky has commented on politics that Marx never influenced, while the words that Lenin took as a sign from Marx are the same politics after his death and continue to create new realities.[3]

In *The Agony of Christianity*, Unamuno praises a phrase attributed to Lenin, pronounced in contradicting someone who claimed that his efforts went against reality: "So much worse for reality!" Marxism, where it has shown itself to be revolutionary—that is, where it has been Marxist—has never obeyed a passive and rigid determinism. The reformists opposed the revolution during the post-war revolutionary wave with the most rudimentary economic determinist arguments—arguments that were, deep down, identified with those of the conservative bourgeoisie and that demonstrated the absolutely bourgeois and non-socialist character of such determinism. To most of its critics, the Russian Revolution appears, on the other hand, as a rationalist, romantic, anti-historical attempt by fanatical utopians. All caliber of reformists primarily rebuked the revolutionaries' tendency to force history, calling the tactics of the parties of the Third International "Blanquist" and "putschist."

Marx could only conceive or propose realistic politics, and he carried to extremes his demonstration that the processes of the capitalist economy lead to socialism to the extent that they are fully and energetically realized. But he understood the spiritual and intellectual training of the proletariat, through the class struggle, as a precondition of a new order. Before Marx, the modern world had already arrived at a time when no political and social doctrine could appear to contradict history and science. The decline of religion has its quite visible origin in its increasing estrangement from historical and scientific experience. And it would be absurd to ask a political conception, eminently modern in all its elements, such as socialism, to be indifferent to this order of consideration. As Brenda observes in his book *The Treason of Intellectuals*, all contemporary political movements, starting with the most reactionary, are characterized by their efforts to attribute to themselves a strict correspondence with the course of history. For the reactionaries of Action Française,[4] who are literally more positivist than any revolutionary, the entire period inaugurated by the liberal revolution is monstrously romantic and antihistorical. The limits and function of Marxist determinism have long been established. Critics oblivious to all party criteria, such as Adriano Tilgher, subscribe to the following interpretation:

> Socialist tactics, to lead to success, must take into account the historical situation in which they must operate, and where it is still immature for the establishment of socialism, refrain from forcing its hand. On the other hand, one should not adopt a quietistic approach regarding the development of events, but rather, insert themselves into this flow to orient these events in a socialist sense so as to make them ripe for the final transformation. Marxist tactics are thus as dynamic and dialectical as Marx's doctrine itself. Socialists do not agitate in a vacuum, do not disregard the preexisting situation, do not delude themselves that they can change things with calls to the good hearts of men; rather, they adhere solidly to historical reality without, however, re-

signing themselves to it. Rather, they energetically re-act against historical reality with the goal of reinforcing the proletariat economically and spiritually, of instilling in them consciousness of their conflict with the bour-geoisie, until, having reached the limit of exasperation, and with the bourgeoisie having reached height of pow-er of the capitalist regime, it becomes an obstacle for the productive forces, and they can be usefully overthrown and replaced by the socialist regime, to the advantage of all.[5]

The voluntarist character of socialism is, in truth, no less evident—despite the fact that it is less under-stood by its critics—than its deterministic back-ground. To assess it, however, it is nevertheless enough to follow the development of the proletarian movement, from the action of Marx and Engels in London at the beginning of the First International to the present, dominated by the first experiment of the socialist state: the USSR. In this process, every word, every Marxist act, resounds with faith, will, heroic and creative conviction, whose impulse it would be absurd to seek in a mediocre and passive determinist sentiment.

Source: *Defensa del Marxismo*

3

THE PROBLEM OF THE INDIAN

Any theses on the Indigenous problem—verbal or written—that fail or refuse to recognize it as a socio-economic problem, are but sterile, theoretical exercises destined to be completely discredited. Their good will is not going to save them. Practically all of them have served only to hide or distort the reality of the problem. Socialist criticism discovers and clarifies it, because it looks for its causes in the country's economy and not in its administrative, legal or ecclesiastical mechanisms, nor in its duality or plurality of races, or in its cultural and moral conditions. The Indigenous question starts in our economy. It has its roots in the land ownership regime. Any attempt to solve it with administrative or enforcement measures, through education or with road building programs, is superficial and secondary as long as the feudalism of the *gamonales*[1] continues to exist.[2]

Gamonalismo necessarily invalidates any law or ordinance of Indigenous protection. The hacienda owner, the *latifundista*,[3] is a feudal lord. The written law is powerless against his authority, which is supported by custom and habit. Unpaid labor is prohibited by law, and yet unpaid labor, and even forced labor, survives on the latifundia. The judge, the subprefect, the commissioner, the teacher, and the tax collector are all in bondage to the landed estate. The law cannot prevail against the *gamonales*. Any official who insists on imposing it, would be abandoned and sacrificed by the central government; here, the influences of *gamonalismo* are all-powerful, acting directly or through parliament with equal effectiveness.

A fresh approach to the Indigenous problem, therefore, ought to be much more concerned with the consequences of the land tenure system than with the guidelines of protective legislation. The new trend was started in 1918 by Dr. Jose A. Encinas in his *Contribución a una legislación tutelar Indígena,* and it has steadily gained strength. But, due to the very nature of his work, Dr. Encinas could not formulate in it an economic-social program. His proposals, aimed at the protection of Indigenous property, had to be limited to this legal objective. Outlining the basics of an Indigenous homestead act, Dr. Encinas recommends the distribution of state and church lands. He did not mention expropriating the land of the latifundium *gamonales. However,* his thesis is distinguished by the repeated denunciation of the effects of *latifundismo,* which in a certain way preludes the current socio-economic critique of the Indigenous question.

This approach repudiates and disqualifies the various theses that consider the issue with one or another of the following unilateral and exclusive criteria: administrative, legal, ethnic, moral, educational, or ecclesiastical.

The oldest and most obvious mistake is, without a doubt, that of reducing the protection of Indigenous people to a matter of ordinary administration. Since the days of Spanish colonial legislation, wise and long-standing ordinances, drawn up after conscientious study, have proved to be completely unsuccessful. The Republic, since independence, has been prolific in its decrees, laws, and provisions intended to protect the Indian against exaction and abuse. The *gamonal* of today, like the *encomendero*[4] of yesterday, nevertheless has very little to fear from administrative theory. He knows that the practice is altogether different.

The individualistic nature of the legislation of the Republic has unquestionably favored the absorption of Indigenous property by the latifundium system. The situation of the Indian, in this respect, was contemplated with greater realism by Spanish legislation. But legal reform has no more practical value than administrative reform, in the face of feudalism intact in its economic structure. The appropriation of most of the Indigenous communal and individual property has already been accomplished. The experience of all the countries that have come out of their feudal era shows us, on the other hand, that without the dissolution of the fiefdom, a liberal law could not function anywhere.

The assumption that the Indigenous problem is an ethnic problem is nourished by the oldest repertoire of imperialist ideas. The concept of the inferior races served the white West in its work of expansion and conquest. To expect Indigenous emancipation from the racial mixing of Indigenous populations with white immigrants is anti-sociological naïveté, conceivable only in the rudimentary mind of an importer of merino sheep. The Asian peoples, to whom Indigenous people are not one iota inferior, have assimilated Western culture in a dynamic and creative way, without transfusions of European blood. The degeneration of the Peruvian Indian is a cheap invention of sophists who serve feudal interests.

The tendency to consider the Indigenous problem as a moral problem embodies a liberal, humanitarian, nineteenth-century Enlightenment conception that encourages and motivates the "leagues of the Rights of Man" in the Western political order. The antislavery conferences and societies, which in Europe have more or less unsuccessfully denounced the crimes of the colonizers, are born of this tendency, which has always relied heavily on its appeals to the moral sense of civilization. González Prada was not exempt from his hope when he wrote that the "condition of the Indigenous can improve in two ways: either the heart of the oppressors is saddened to the point of recognizing the right of the oppressed, or the spirit of the oppressed acquires manhood enough to chastise the oppressors."[5] The Pro-Indigenous Association (1909-1917) represented, above all, the same hope, although its true effectiveness lay in the concrete and immediate measures taken by its directors in defense of the Indian—an orientation that owes much to the practical, and characteristically Saxon, idealism of Dora Mayer. The experiment of the Association has become widely known in Peru and in the rest of the world. Humanitarian preaching has neither stopped nor embarrassed imperialist in Europe, nor has it reformed their methods. The struggle against imperialism now relies solely on the solidarity and strength of the liberation movements of the colonial masses. This concept presides in contemporary European anti-imperialist action, action that is supported by liberals like Albert Einstein and Romain Rolland and, therefore, cannot be considered exclusively socialist.

In the field of reason and morality, religious action had a grater energy, or at least a greater authority, centuries ago. However, this crusade obtained only very wisely inspired laws and provisions. The fortune of the Indians did not substantially change. Gonzalez Prada, whose point of view, as we know, was not strictly socialist, sought the explanation for this failure in the economic core of the question:

> It could not have happened otherwise; the exploitation of the defeated was officially ordered; it was pretended that evils were humanely perpetrated and injustices committed equitably. To eradicate abuses, it would have been necessary to abolish land appropriation and forced labor, in brief, to change the entire colonial regime. Without the toil of the American Indian, the coffers of the Spanish treasury would have been emptied.[6]

In any event, religious tenets were more likely to succeed than liberal tenets. The former appealed to a noble and active Spanish Catholicism, whereas the latter tried to make itself heard by a weak and formalist *criollo* liberalism.

But today a religious solution is unquestionably the most backward and anti-historical of all. Those who

represent it—unlike their so very distant teachers—
are not concerned with obtaining a new declaration of
Indigenous rights, with adequate authorities and ordinances. Rather, the missionary is assigned the role
of mediator between the Indian and the *gamonal*. If
the church could not accomplish its task in a medieval
era, when its spiritual and intellectual capacity could
be measured by friars like Las Casas,[7] how can it succeed with the elements it commands today? The Sev-
enth-Day Adventists, in that respect, have taken the
lead from the Catholic clergy, whose cloisters daily
attract fewer and fewer evangelists.

The belief that the problem of the Indian is one of
education does not seem to be supported by even a
strictly and independently pedagogical criterion. Today, education takes social and economic factors into
account more than ever. The modern pedagogue
knows perfectly well that education is not a mere
question of school and teaching methods. Economic
and social circumstances necessarily condition the
work of the teacher. *Gamonalismo* is fundamentally
opposed to the education of the Indian; it has the same
interest in keeping the Indian ignorant as it has in en-
couraging him to depend on alcohol. The modern
school—assuming that in the present situation it
could be multiplied at the same rate as the rural
school-age population—is incompatible with the feudal latifundium. The mechanics of Indigenous servitude would completely nullify the actions of the
school if the latter, by a miracle that is inconceivable
within social reality, should manage to preserve its
pedagogical mission under a feudal regime. The most
efficient and grandiose teaching system could not per-

form these miracles. The school and the teacher are inevitably condemned to become denatured under the pressure of the feudal environment, which cannot be reconciled with the most elementary concept of progress and evolution. When this truth becomes partially understood, the saving formula is thought to be discovered in boarding schools for Indians. But the glaring inadequacy of this formula is self-evident in view of the tiny percentage of the Indigenous school population that can be boarded in these schools.

The pedagogical solution, advocated by many in good faith, is now officially ruled out. Educators, I repeat, can least afford to ignore economic and social reality. At present, it only exists as a vague and formless suggestion which no body or doctrine wants to adopt.

The new approach locates the Indigenous problem in the land tenure system.

Note 1: In my prologue to Valcarcel's *Tempestad en los Andes*, an impassioned and militant champion of the Indian, I have explained my point of view as follows:

"Faith in the renaissance of the Indian is not pinned to the material process of 'Westernizing' the Quechua country. The soul of the Indian is not raised by the white man's civilization or alphabet but by the myth, the idea, of the Socialist revolution. The hope of the Indian is absolutely revolutionary. That same myth, that same idea, are the decisive agents in the awakening of other ancient peoples or races in ruin: the people of India, the Chinese, etc. Universal history today tends as never before to chart its course with a common quadrant. Why should the Inca people, who constructed the most highly-developed and harmonious communistic system, be the only ones unmoved by this worldwide emotion? The consanguinity of the Indian movement with world revolutionary currents is too evident to need documentation. I have said already that I reached an understanding and appreciation of the Indian through socialism. The case of Valcarcel proves the validity of my personal experience. Valcarcel, a man with a different intellectual background, influenced by traditionalist tastes and oriented by another type of guidance and studies, politically resolved his concern for the Indian in socialism. In this book, he tells us that 'the Indigenous proletariat awaits its Lenin. A Marxist would not state it differently.

"As long as the vindication of the Indian is kept on a philosophical and cultural plane, it lacks a concrete historical base. To acquire such a base— that is, to acquire physical reality—it must be converted into an economic and political vindication. Socialism has taught us how to present the Indigenous problem in new terms. We have ceased to consider it abstractly as an ethnic or moral problem and we now recognize it concretely as a social, economic, and political problem. And, for the first time, we have felt it to be clearly defined.

"Those who have not yet broken free of the limitations of a liberal bourgeois education take an abstractionist and literary position. They idly discuss the racial aspects of the problem, disguising its reality under a pseudo-idealistic language and forgetting that it is essentially dominated by politics and, therefore, by economics. They counter revolutionary dialectics with a confused critical jargon, according to which a political reform or event cannot solve the Indian problem because its immediate effects would not reach a multitude of complicated customs and vices that can only be changed through a long and normal evolutionary process.

"History, fortunately, dispels all doubts and clears up all ambiguities. The conquest was a political event. Although it abruptly interrupted the autonomous evolution of the Quechua nation, it did not involve a sudden substitution of the conquerors' law and customs for those of the natives. Nevertheless, this political event opened up a new period in every aspect of their spiritual and material existence. The change in regime altered the life of the Quechua people to its very foundations. Independence was another political event. It, too, did not bring about a radical transformation in the economic and social structure of Peru; but it initiated, notwithstanding, another period of our history. Although it did not noticeably improve the condition of the Indian, having hardly touched the colonial economic infrastructure, it did change his legal situation and clear the way for his political and social emancipation. If the republic did not continue along this road, the fault lies entirely with the class that profited from independence, which was potentially very rich in values and creative principles.

"The problem of the Indian must no longer be obscured and confused by the perpetual arguments of the throng of lawyers and writers who are consciously or unconsciously in league with the *latifundistas*. The moral and material misery of the Indian is too clearly the result of the economic and social system that has oppressed him for centuries. This system, which succeeded colonial feudalism, is *Gamonalismo*. While it rules supreme, there can be no question of redeeming the Indian.

"The term *Gamonalismo* designates more than just a social and economic category: that of the *latifundistas* or large landowners. It signifies a whole phenomenon. *Gamonalismo* is represented not only by the *gamonales* but by a long hierarchy of officials, intermediaries, agents, parasites, et cetera. The literate Indian who enters the service of *Gamonalismo* turns into an exploiter of his own race. The central factor of the phenomenon is the hegemony of the semi-feudal landed estate in the policy and inner workings of the government. Therefore, it is this factor that should be acted upon if the evil is to be attacked at its roots and not merely observed in its temporary or subsidiary manifestations.

"*Gamonalismo* or feudalism could have been eliminated by the republic within its liberal and capitalist principles. But for reasons I have already indicated, those principles have not effectively and fully directed our historic process. They were sabotaged by the very class charged with applying them and for more than a century they have been powerless to rescue the Indian from a servitude that was an integral part of the feudal system. It cannot be hoped that today, when those principles are in crisis all over the world, they can suddenly acquire in Peru an unwonted creative vitality.

"Revolutionary and even reformist thought can no longer be liberal; they must be socialist. Socialism appears in our history not because of chance, imitation, or fashion, as some superficial minds would believe, but because it was historically inevitable. On the one hand, we who profess socialism struggle logically and consistently for the reorganization of our country on socialist bases; proving that the economic and political regime that we oppose has turned into an instrument for colonizing the country on behalf of capitalist imperialism, we declare that this is a moment in our history when it is impossible to be really nationalist and revolutionary without being socialist. On the other hand, there does not exist and never has existed in Peru a progressive bourgeoisie, endowed with national sentiments, that claims to be liberal and democratic and that derives its policy from the postulates of its doctrine."

Source: *7 Ensayos de Interpretación de la Realidad Peruana.*

4

THE PROBLEM OF RACE IN LATIN AMERICA

Approaching the Issue

In bourgeois intellectual speculation, the problem of race in Latin America serves, among other things, to cover up or ignore the true problems of the continent. Marxist criticism has an urgent obligation to state it in its real terms, detaching it from any casuist or pedantic misrepresentation. Economically, socially, and politically, the problem of race, like that of land, is, at its base, that of the liquidation of feudalism.

The Indigenous races in Latin America are in a clamorous state of backwardness and ignorance, due to the servitude that weighs on them, since the Spanish conquest. The interest of the exploiting class, first the Spanish and later the creole, has invariably tended, under various guises, to explain the condition of the Indigenous races with the argument of their inferiority or primitivism. By employing this, that class has done nothing but reproduce the reasoning of the white race on the issue of the treatment and care of the colonial peoples in the national debate on this issue.

The sociologist Vilfredo Pareto, who reduces race to just one of the several factors that determine the forms of the development of a society, has judged the hypocrisy of the idea of race in the imperialist and enslavement policies of white people in the following terms:

> Aristotle's theory of natural slavery is also the theory put forward by modern civilized peoples to justify their conquests of peoples whom they call inferior and their domination over them. Aristotle said that some men are naturally slaves and others masters, and that it is proper for the former to obey and the others to command, which is just and of benefit to all concerned. So say the modern peoples who decorate themselves with the title "civilized." They assert that there are people—themselves, of course—who were intended by nature to rule, and other peoples, those whom they wish to exploit, who were no less intended by nature to obey, and that it is just, proper, and to the advantage of everyone concerned that they do the ruling and the others the obeying. Whence it follows that if an Englishman, a German, a Frenchman, a Belgian, an Italian, fights and dies for his country, he is a hero; but if an African dares to defend his homeland against these nations, he is a contemptible rebel and traitor. So the Europeans are preforming a sacrosanct duty in exterminating Africans in an effort to teach them to be civilized. And there are always plenty of people to admire such work "of peace, progress, and civilization," with mouths agape! It is necessary to add that, with truly admirable hypocrisy, these blessed civilized people claim to be acting for the good of their sub-

ject races when they oppress, and even exterminate, them; and they dedicate so much love to them that they want them "free" by force. Thus the English freed the Indians from the "tyranny" of the Raja, the Germans freed the Africans from the "tyranny" of the black kings, the Italians liberated the Arabs from the oppression of the Turks, the French freed the inhabitants of Madagascar and, to make them freer still, they killed many and reduced the others to a state of slavery in all but name. Such talk is said in all seriousness and there are even those who believe it. The cat catches the mouse and eats it, but it doesn't say it does so for the mouse's sake. It does not proclaim a dogma of the equality of all animals nor hypocritically raise its eyes to heaven in worship the Father of us all.[1]

The exploitation of Indigenous people in Latin America is also justified on the pretext that it serves the cultural and moral redemption of the oppressed races.

Meanwhile, as it is easy to prove, the colonization of Latin America by the white race has only had a delaying and depressing effect on the lives of the Indigenous races. The natural evolution of these people has been interrupted by the degrading oppression of whites and mestizos. Peoples such as the Quechua and Aztecs, who had reached an high degree of social organization, reverted, under the colonial regime, to the condition of dispersed agricultural tribes. The elements of civilization that remain in the Indigenous communities of Peru are, above all, what survives of the ancient autochthonous organization. With a feudal agricultural system, white civilization has not created pockets of urban life, much less industrialization and mechanization. In the highland *latifundios*,[2] with the exception of certain cattle ranches, white domination does not represent, even technologically, any progress with respect to aboriginal culture.

What we call the Indigenous problem is the feudal exploitation of the natives on the large agrarian properties. The Indian, in 90 percent of the cases, is not a proletarian but a serf. Capitalism, as an economic and political system, is incapable of building an economy emancipated from feudal flaws in Latin America. The perception of the inferiority of the Indigenous race allows for a maximum exploitation of the workers of this race. Those that benefit from it are unwilling to give up this advantage. In agriculture, the establishment of wages and the adoption of the machine, do not erase the feudal character of the large landholdings. They simply perfect the system of exploitation of the land and the peasant masses. Many of our bourgeois and *gamonales* warmly support the thesis of the inferiority of the Indian. The Indigenous problem is, in their opinion, an ethnic problem whose solution depends on the crossing of the Indigenous race with superior foreign races. The subsistence of a feudal-based economy is presented, however, in irreconcilable opposition with an immigration movement sufficient to produce this transformation by crossing. The wages paid on the coastal and highland estates (when wages are adopted in the latter) rule out the possibility of employing European immigrants in agriculture. Peasant immigrants would never come to work under the conditions of the Indians; they would only be attracted to this work by making them small landowners. The Indian could never be replaced in the agricultural tasks of the coastal estates but with the black slave or the Chinese "coolies." The colonization plans for European immigrants are, for now, exclusively in the wooded region of the East known as the Montaña. The thesis that the Indigenous problem is an ethnic problem does not even deserve to be discussed, but it should be noted to what extent the solution proposed is at odds with the interests and possibilities of the bourgeoisie and the *gamonalismo*, in whom it finds its adherents.

For Yankee and English imperialism, the economic value of these naturally rich lands would be much less if they did not possess a backward and miserable Indigenous population, which is extremely exploitable with the help of the national bourgeoisie. The history of the Peruvian sugar industry, currently in crisis, shows that its profits have rested, above all, on the cheapness of labor, that is, on the misery of the laborers. Technically, this industry has never been in a position to compete with that of other countries on the world market. The distance from the consumer markets burdened their exports with high freight costs. But all these disadvantages were largely compensated by the cheapness of the workforce. The work of enslaved peasant masses, housed in disgusting shanties, deprived of all freedom and rights, subjected to an overwhelming journey, placed Peruvian sugar producers in a position to compete with those who, in other countries, cultivated their lands better or were protected by a protectionist tariff or more advantageously located from a geographical point of view. Foreign capitalism uses the feudal class to exploit these peasant masses to its advantage. More often than not, the inability of these large landowners (heirs of prejudice, medieval arrogance, and arbitrariness) to fill the function of heads of capitalist companies, is such that they are forced to take the administration of large estates and plants into their own hands. This is particularly the case in the sugar industry, monopolized almost entirely in the Chicama Valley by an English and a German company.

Race, above all, has great importance in regards to imperialism. But it also has another role that prevents the struggle for national independence in Latin American countries that have a high percentage of Indigenous population from being seen as parallel to the same problem in Asia or Africa. The feudal or bourgeois elements in our countries feel the same contempt for the Indians, Blacks, and mulattos, as the white imperialists. Racial sentiment operates in this ruling class in a way absolutely favorable to imperialist penetration. Between the lord or the creole bourgeois and his colored pawns, there is nothing in common. Class solidarity is added to the solidarity of race or prejudice to make the national bourgeoisie docile instruments of Yankee or British imperialism. And this sentiment extends to a large part of the middle classes, which imitate the aristocracy and the bourgeoisie in disdain for the colored commons, even though their own miscegenation is too evident.

The black race, imported into Latin America by the colonizers to increase their power over the American Indian race, passively filled its colonialist role. Themselves harshly exploited, they reinforced the oppression of the Indigenous race by the Spanish conquerors. A greater degree of mixing, familiarity and coexistence with them in the colonial cities, made the black race an auxiliary to white dominance, notwithstanding any rush of their turbulent or restless spirit. Blacks or mulattos, in their role as artisans or domestic servants, composed a plebeian class that was always more or less unconditionally disposed to the feudal class. Industry, factories, and unions redeem black people from this domesticity. In erasing racial boundaries between proletarians, class consciousness historically has raised black morale. The union means the definitive rupture of the servile habits that otherwise would keep Blacks at the level of craftsman or servant.

The Indian is in no way inferior to the *mestizo* in their ability to assimilate progress of the modern techniques of production. On the contrary, they are generally superior. The idea of their racial inferiority is currently too discredited to deserve the honors of a refutation. White and creole prejudice toward perceived inferiority is not based on any facts worth taking into consideration in a scientific study of the question. Coca addiction and alcoholism of the Indigenous race, greatly exaggerated by its commentators, are nothing but consequences, results of white oppression. *Gamonalismo* encourages and exploits these vices, which in a way are fed by the need to fight against pain that is particularly alive and active in a subjugated people. The Indian in ancient times only drank "chicha," a fermented corn drink, whereas it was the whites who implanted the cultivation of sugarcane and alcohol production on the continent. The production of cane alcohol is one of the most "healthy" and secure businesses for large landholders, in whose hands also lies the production of coca in the warm mountain valleys.

Long ago, the Japanese experience demonstrated the ease with which peoples of race and traditions distinct from Europe took to western science and adapted to the use of its productive techniques. In the mines and factories of the Peruvian highlands, the Indian peasant confirms this experience.

And Marxist sociology has already summarily dismissed racist ideas that are products of the imperialist spirit. Bukharin writes in *Historical Materialism*:

In the first place, the race theory is in contradiction with the facts. The "lowest" race, that which is said to be incapable, by nature, of any development, is the black race, the Negroes. Yet it has been shown that the ancient representatives of this black race, the so called Kushites, created a very high civilization in India (before the days of the Hindus) and Egypt; the yellow race, which now also enjoys but slight favor, also created a high civilization in China, far superior in its day to the then existing civilizations of white men; the white men were then children as compared with the yellow men. We now know how much the ancient Greeks borrowed from the Assyro-Babylonians and the Egyptians. These few facts are sufficient to show that the "racial" explanation is no explanation at all. It may be replied: perhaps you were right, but will you go so far as to say that the average Negro stands at the same level, in his abilities, as the average European? There is no sense in answering such a question with benevolent subterfuges, as certain liberal professors sometimes do, to the effect that all men are of course equal, that according to Kant, the human personality is in itself a final consideration, or that Christ taught that there are no Hellenes, or Jews, etc. To aspire to equality between races is one thing; to admit the similarity of their qualities is another. We aspire to that which does not exist; otherwise we are attempting to force doors that are already open. We are now not concerned with the question: what must be our aim? We are considering the question of whether there is a difference between the level, cultural and otherwise, of white men and black men, on the whole. There is such a difference; the "white" men are at present on a higher level, but this only goes to show that at present these so called races have changed places.

This is a complete refutation of the theory of race. At, bottom, this theory always reduces itself to the peculiarities of races, to their immemorial "character." If such were the case, this "character" would have expressed itself in the same way in all the periods of history. The obvious inference is that the "nature" of the races is constantly changing with the conditions of their existence. But these conditions are determined by nothing more nor less than the relation between society and nature, i.e, the condition of the productive forces. In other words, the theory of race does not in the slightest manner explain the conditions of social evolution. Here also it is evident that the analysis must begin with the movement of the productive forces.[3]

From the assumption of the inferiority of the Indigenous race, one begins to pass to the opposite extreme: that the creation of a new American culture will be essentially the work of the Indigenous racial forces alone. To subscribe to this thesis is to fall into the most naive and absurd mysticism. It would be foolish and dangerous to oppose the racism of those who despise the Indian because they believe in the absolute and permanent superiority of the white race with the overestimation of the Indian with messianic faith in their mission as a race in the American renaissance.

The possibilities for the Indian to rise materially and intellectually depend on changes in socioeconomic conditions. They are not determined by race but by economy and politics. Race by itself has not awakened nor will it awaken the understanding of an emancipatory ideal. Above all, it will never acquire the power to impose and carry it out. What ensures their emancipation is the dynamism of an economy and a culture that carries within it the germ of socialism. The Indian race was not defeated in the war of conquest by an ethnically or qualitatively superior race; it was defeated by technology that was far above the technology of aboriginal people. Gunpowder, iron, and cavalry were not *racial* advantages; they were *technical* advantages. The Spanish arrived in these distant regions because they had means of navigation that allowed them to cross oceans. Navigation and trade later allowed them to exploit some of the natural resources of their colonies. Spanish feudalism superimposed itself over Indigenous agrarianism, although it did in part respect its communal structures. But this very adaptation created a static order, an economic system whose factors of stagnation were the best guarantee of Indigenous servitude. Capitalist industry breaks this equilibrium, disrupts this stagnation by creating new productive forces and new relations of production. The proletariat grows gradually at the expense of artisanship and servitude. The economic and social evolution of the nation enters an era of activity and contradictions that, on an ideological level, causes the emergence and development of socialist thought.

In all this, the influence of the race factor is evidently secondary to the influence of the economic factors
—production, technology, science, etc. Would it be
possible to outline the plan or intentions of a socialist
state based on demands for the emancipation of the
Indigenous masses without addressing the material
elements of modern industry or, if you like, capitalism? The dynamism of this economy, of this regime,
which renders all relations unstable, and which sets
ideologies and classes in opposition, is undoubtedly
what makes the Indigenous resurrection feasible. The
play of economic, political, cultural, ideological
forces, not racial ones, is what decides this reality. The
greatest charge against the ruling class of the republic
is its failure to accelerate, with a more liberal, bourgeois, more capitalist intelligence of its mission, the
process of transformation of the colonial economy into a capitalist economy. Feudalism opposes emancipation, the awakening of Indigenous peoples from
their stagnation and inertia. Capitalism, with its conflicts and its own instruments of exploitation, advances the thinking of the masses and their demands,
forcing a struggle in which they are materially and
mentally trained to preside over a new order.

The problem of race is not common to all Latin
American countries, nor does it present the same proportions and characteristics in all those who suffer
from it. In some Latin American countries it is more
localized or regional and does not appreciably influence social and economic processes. But in countries
like Peru and Bolivia, and somewhat less in Ecuador,
where the majority of the population is Indigenous,
the Indian's demands are the dominant popular and

social demands.

In these countries the race factor is compounded by the class factor in a way that revolutionary politics cannot fail to take into account. The Quechua or Aymara Indian sees his oppressor in the *mestizo* and the white person. And in the *mestizo*, only class consciousness is capable of destroying the habit of contempt, of disgust for the Indian. It is not uncommon to find prejudice against the Indian or the resistance to recognize this prejudice as a simple inheritance or mental contagion of the environment among the very urban elements who proclaim to be revolutionary.

The language barrier stands between the Indian peasant masses and the white or *mestizo* nuclei of revolutionary workers. But, through Indian propagandists, the socialist doctrine, by the nature of its demands, will soon take root in the Indigenous masses. What has been lacking until now is the systematic preparation of these propagandists. Literate Indians, corrupted by the city, regularly become accessories to the exploiters of their race. But in the city, in the revolutionary working-class environment, the Indian is already beginning to assimilate the revolutionary idea, to appropriate it, to understand its value as an instrument for the emancipation of their race, which is oppressed by the same class that exploits the worker in the factory, whom the Indigenous workers discover to be a class brother.

The realism of a safe and precise socialist policy for assessing and using the facts on which they have to act in these countries can and must turn the race factor into a revolutionary factor. The current state structures in these countries rest on the alliance of the feudal landowning class and the mercantile bourgeoisie. Once this landed feudalistic structure is defeated, urban capitalism will lack the strength to resist the rise of the workers. It is represented by a mediocre and weak bourgeoisie, formed in privilege, without a combative and organized spirit that daily loses its ascendancy over the fluctuating intellectual caste.

Socialist criticism in Peru has initiated a new approach to the Indigenous problem with the inexorable denunciation and rejection of all bourgeois or philanthropic tendencies to consider race as an administrative, legal, moral, religious or educational problem.[4] The economic and political terms on which this issue and the proletarian struggle to resolve it are raised in Peru, and by analogy in other Latin American countries with large Indigenous populations, in our opinion are the following:

1. Socioeconomic Situation of the Indigenous Population of Peru

There is no recent census that allows us to know exactly the current size of the Indigenous population. It is generally accepted that the Indigenous race makes up four-fifths of a total population calculated at a minimum of 5,000,000. This assessment does not strictly take race into account, but rather the socioeconomic condition of the masses that make up these four fifths. There are provinces where the Indigenous typology shows an extensive intermixing. But in these sectors, white blood has been completely assimilated by the Indigenous environment and the life of the *cholos*[5] produced by this miscegenation does not differ from the life of the Indians themselves.

No less than 90 percent of the Indigenous population work in agriculture. The development of the mining industry has recently resulted in the increasing use of Indigenous labor in mining. But part of the mining workers are still farmers. They are "community"[6] Indians who spend most of the year in the mines, but at the time of agricultural work return to their small plots that are insufficient for subsistence.

Today, a feudal or semi-feudal work system still exists in agriculture. In the haciendas of the Sierra, wage labor, when it exists, appears so incipient and deformed that it hardly alters the features of the feudal regime. Indians typically do not obtain but a petty part of the fruits for their labor.[7] The soil is worked in a primitive way in almost all the large estates. Even though those estates always keep the best lands, in many cases their yields are lower than that of the Indigenous communities. In some regions Indigenous communities retain part of the land but in meager proportion to their needs so that their members are obliged to work for the large landowners.

These estate owners, owners of vast tracts of largely uncultivated land, in many cases have not stripped the communities of their traditional properties because if a community is attached to an estate, it can then securely count on its "*own*" labor supply. The value of a large estate is calculated not only from its territorial extension, but *from its own Indigenous population*. When an estate does not have this population, the owner, in accord with the authorities, resorts to the *forced recruitment* of poorly paid peons. Indians of both sexes, including children, are obliged to provide free services to owners and their families, as well as to the authorities. Men, women and children take turns in the service of the *gamonales* and authorities, not only in the hacienda houses, but in the towns or cities in which they reside. The provision of free services has been legally prohibited several times; but in practice it remains to this day, because no law can counteract the mechanics of the feudal order as long as this structure remains intact. Recently, the road conscription law has accentuated the feudal structure of the highlands. This law requires all individuals to work six days every six months in the building or maintenance of roads or to "redeem" themselves by paying taxes according to the established rate in each region. In many cases Indians are forced to work long distances from their homes, which forces them to sacrifice a greater number of days. Road conscription, which for the Indigenous masses has the character of the old colonial *mitas*,[8] provides the authorities with pretext to plunder.

Wage labor prevails in the mines. In the Junín and La Libertad mines, where the two large mining companies (the Cerro de Pasco Copper Corporation and the "Northern," respectively) exploit copper, the workers earn wages of 2.50 to 3.00 soles. These wages are undoubtedly high compared to the unbelievably low wages (twenty or thirty cents) that are customary in the highland estates. But companies take advantage of the backward condition of Indigenous peoples in all forms. The current social legislation is virtually null in the mines, where the laws on work accidents and eight-hour days are not observed, nor is the right of association recognized for workers. Every worker accused of attempting to organize the workers, even if only for cultural or mutual purposes, is immediately fired by the company.

The companies usually employ "contractors" to the work in the galleries who, in order to carry out the work at the lowest cost, act as an instrument of exploitation of the manual workers. The "contractors," however, typically live in austere conditions, overwhelmed by the obligations to repay their advances which make them permanent debtors of the companies. When an accident at work occurs, companies use their lawyers to dodge their responsibilities, abusing the misery and ignorance of Indigenous people to deny them their rights, paying them arbitrary and miserable wages. The Morococha disaster, which cost the lives of a few dozen workers, has recently lead to the denunciation of the insecurity in which the miners work. The poor condition of some tunnels and work that almost touched the bottom of a pond, caused a collapse that left many workers buried. Officially, there were 27 victims, but there are reports that the number was greater. The allegations of some newspapers led the company to be more respectful of the law than usual in regard to legal compensation to the victims' families. Finally, in order to avoid further unrest, the Cerro de Pasco Copper Corporation has granted its workers a 10 percent increase as long as the current copper price continues to hold. In remote provinces like Cotabambas, the situation of the miners is much more backward and distressing. The *gamonales* of the region are in charge of the forced recruitment of Indians, and the wages are miserable.

Industry has barely penetrated the Sierra. It is represented mainly by the fabric factories of Cuzco, where the production of excellent qualities of wool is the main factor in its development. With the exception of the management and bosses, the working staff of these factories are entirely Indigenous. The Indian has been perfectly assimilated to mechanization. They are careful and sober operators whom the capitalist skillfully exploits. The feudal atmosphere of agriculture extends to these factories, where a certain patriarchalism uses the proteges and wards of the master as instruments for the subjugation of their colleagues and to oppose the formation of class consciousness.

In recent years, a rise in the prices of Peruvian wool in foreign markets has initiated a process of industrialization of southern agricultural estates. Several landowners have introduced modern technology, importing foreign livestock that have improved the volume and quality of production, shaking off the yoke of commercial intermediaries, and establishing mills and other small industrial plants on their farms. Apart from this, in the highlands there are no more industrial plants and crops other than those used for the production of sugar, molasses, and liquor for regional consumption.

Indigenous highland labor is used to a considerable extent for the operation of the coastal haciendas where the population is insufficient. Large sugar and cotton estates use *enganchadores* [labor recruiters] to supply the necessary laborers for their agricultural activities. These workers earn wages that, though always very meager, are higher than wages typically paid in the feudal highlands. But in return they suffer from strenuous work in a warm climate, a diet inadequate for the job, and malaria, which is endemic in the coastal valleys. Its hard for the highland peon to escape malaria, which forces them to return to their region, often with an incurable case of tuberculosis as well.

Although agriculture in these estates is industrialized (the land is worked with modern methods and machines and the products are processed in "mills" or well-equipped plants), the environment is not that of capitalism and wage labor in urban industry. This system retains its feudal spirit and practice in the treatment of workers. Estate owners do not *recognize* the rights established by labor laws. On these *haciendas* there is no law other than that of the owner. No shadow of workers' association is tolerated. Employees deny entry to individuals who, for any reason, mistrust the owner or manager. During the colonial period, these *haciendas* were worked with Black slaves. Once slavery was abolished, they brought in Chinese coolies. The traditional landowner has not lost their habits of slave trader or feudal lord.

In the forests of the montaña region, agriculture is still nascent. It uses the same enganche[9] system used in the highlands, and to some extent uses the services of tribes familiar with whites. But in terms of work regime, the montaña has a far grimmer tradition. The most barbarous and criminal slavery procedures were applied in the exploitation of rubber when this product was selling for a high price. The crimes of Putumayo, sensationally denounced by the foreign press, constitute the blackest page in the history of rubber tappers. It is alleged that much about these crimes was exaggerated and fantasized abroad and that an attempt to blackmail was at the origin of the scandal. But the truth is perfectly documented by the investigations and testimonies of Peruvian justice officials such as Judge Valcárcel and Prosecutor Paredes who verified the slaving and bloodthirsty methods of the Araos overseers. Less than three years ago, an outstanding official, Dr. Chuquihuanca Ayulo, a great defender of the Indigenous race—Indigenous himself —was relieved of his duties as prosecutor in the Department of Madre de Dios as a consequence of denouncing the slave-like methods of the most powerful company in that region.

This summary description of the economic and social conditions of the Indigenous population of Peru establishes that alongside a small number of wage-earning miners and a still incipient system of agricultural wage-labor there is a system of servitude. In the distant montaña regions, the Aboriginals are frequently subjected to a system of slavery.

2. The Indigenous Struggle Against *Gamonalismo*

When talking about the attitude of the Indians toward their exploiters, the impression is generally that debased and oppressed Indians are incapable of any form of struggle or resistance. The long history of Indigenous insurrections and riots, and the subsequent massacres and repressions, alone is enough to disprove this impression. In most cases, the uprisings of Indians have originated from violence that incidentally forced them to revolt against a particular authority or a landowner. But in other cases it has not had this character of a local mutiny. The rebellion has followed less incidental upheaval and has spread to a more or less extensive region. To repress uprisings, it has been necessary to appeal to substantial forces and true massacres. Thousands of rebellious Indians have spread fear in the *gamonales* in the provinces. Army Major Teodomiro Gutiérrez, a highland mestizo with a high percentage of Indigenous blood who called himself Rumimaqui and presented himself as the redeemer of his race, led one of the recent uprisings that assumed extraordinary proportions. The Billinghurst government sent Major Gutiérrez to the Puno department,[10] where the *gamonalismo* carried out exploitation to an extreme, to carry out an investigation into the Indigenous complaints and inform the government. Gutiérrez then entered into intimate contact with the Indians. With the Billinghurst government overthrown, he thought that all prospect of legal claims had disappeared and he launched a revolt. Several thousand Indians followed him, but, as always unarmed and defenseless against the troops, were condemned to dispersal or death. This uprising has been followed by those of La Mar and Huancané in 1923 and other minor uprisings—all of them bloodily repressed.

In 1921, delegations from various community groups attended an Indigenous congress held under government auspices. The purpose of the congress was to formulate the claims of the Indigenous race. In Quechua, delegates delivered strong accusations against the *gamonales*, authorities, and priests. They created a Tawantinsuyu[11] Indigenous Rights Committee. Annual congresses were held until 1924, when the government persecuted the revolutionary Indigenous elements, intimidated the delegations, and distorted the spirit and purpose of the assembly.

The 1923 Congress, which voted for conclusions that were disturbing for *gamonalismo*, such as calling for the separation of church and state and repeal of the road conscription law, revealed the danger of these conferences in which groups of Indigenous communities of various regions came into contact and coordinated their action. That same year, Indians formed the Regional Indigenous Workers' Federation with the intent to apply the principles and methods of anarcho-syndicalism to the organization. It was, therefore, destined not to succeed. But it nevertheless represented a revolutionary orientation of the Indigenous vanguard. With two of the Indian leaders of this movement exiled and others intimidated, the Regional Indigenous Workers Federation was soon reduced to just a name. And in 1927 the government declared the Tawantinsuyu Indigenous Rights Committee dissolved, on the pretext that its leaders were mere exploiters of the race that they *claimed* to defend. This committee never had more importance than that attached to its participation in Indigenous congresses. It was made up of elements that lacked ideological and personal valor, and on many occasions had protested in adherence to government policy, considering them to be in favor of the Indians. But for some *gamonales,* it was still an instrument of agitation, a remnant of the Indigenous congresses. The government, on the other hand, directed its policy in the direction of associating with pro-Indigenous declarations, promises of land distribution, etc. This was a resolute act against any agitation among the Indians by revolutionary groups or those susceptible of revolutionary influence.

The penetration of socialist ideas and the expression of revolutionary demands among the Indigenous people have continued despite these vicissitudes. In 1927, a pro-Indigenous action group called Grupo Resurgimiento [Resurgence Group] was founded in Cuzco. It was composed of several intellectuals and artists, along with some Cuzco workers. This group published a manifesto denouncing the crimes of *gamonalismo*.[12] Shortly after its creation, one of its main leaders, Dr. Luis E. Valcárcel, was arrested in Arequipa. His imprisonment lasted only a few days, but meanwhile, the Grupo Resurgimiento was definitively dissolved by the Cuzco authorities.

3. Conclusions on the Indigenous Problem and the Tasks Involved

The Indigenous problem is identified with the land problem. The ignorance, backwardness and misery of the Indigenous people are, we repeat, only the consequence of their servitude. The feudal *latifundio* maintains the absolute exploitation and domination of the Indigenous masses by the landowning class. The struggle of the Indians against the *gamonales* has invariably been in the defense of their lands against absorption and dispossession. There is, therefore, an instinctive and profound Indigenous demand: the demand for land. Giving an organized, systematic, defined character to this demand is the task that we have the duty to actively carry out.

The communities that have demonstrated a truly

amazing persistence and resistance under the harshest oppression represent a natural factor for socialization of the land in Peru. The Indian has an ingrained habit of cooperation. Even when community ownership passes to individual ownership, cooperation is maintained and the heavy work is shared. This is true not only in the highlands, but also on the coast, where a higher level of mixing acts against Indigenous customs. With minimal effort, the community can become a cooperative. Awarding *latifundios* to the communities is the solution to the agrarian problem in the highlands. On the coast, where large landholders are also omnipotent but where communal ownership has disappeared, the inevitable tendency is to the individualization of land ownership. The harshly exploited tenants known as *yanaconas*[13] should be supported in their struggles against the landowners. The natural demand of these *yanaconas* is to own the land they work. The struggle is different on large estates that owners exploit directly with peon labor they recruit partly in the highlands among those that lack a link to the land. The demands for which they must work are: freedom of association, abolition of *enganche*, wage increases, the eight-hour day, and enforcement of protective labor laws. Only when the peons of these estates have won these demands will they be on the path to final emancipation.

It is very difficult for union propaganda to penetrate the haciendas. Each estate, on the coast as in the highlands, is a fiefdom. No association is tolerated that does not accept the patronage and guardianship of the owners and management, and only the sport or recreational associations are found on estates. But with the increase in automobile traffic, a gap gradually opens in the barriers that previously closed the hacienda to all propaganda. This points to the importance of organizing and actively mobilizing transportation workers in the development of the class movement in Peru.

When the peons of the estates know that they have the fraternal solidarity of the unions and understand the value of the unions, it will easily awaken in them the will to fight that today is missing but that more than once they have proven exists. The nuclei of labor union members that are gradually formed on the estates will have the function of explaining to the masses their rights, of defending their interests, of effectively representing them in any claim, and of taking advantage of the first opportunity to shape their organization to the degree circumstances permit.

For the progressive ideological education of the Indigenous masses, the workers' vanguard has those militant elements of the Indian race who, in the mines or urban centers, come into contact with the union and political movements. Their principles are assimilated and they are trained to play a role in the emancipation of their race. Workers from an Indigenous milieu often return temporarily or permanently to their communities. Their language allows them to effectively fulfill a mission as instructors of their race and class brothers. Indian peasants will only understand individuals who speak their own language. They distrust whites and *mestizos*, and, in turn the whites and the *mestizos* distrust the Indians.

Methods of self-education, regular reading of the periodicals and of the union and revolutionary movement in Latin America, and correspondence with comrades in the urban centers will be the means by which the Indigenous masses will successfully complete their educational mission.

Indigenous members of our movement must always take a principal and leading role in various activities with the dual objective of giving a serious direction to the class orientation and education of Indigenous peoples and avoiding the influence of misleading elements (anarchists, demagogues, reformers, etc.). Activities also include coordination of Indigenous communities by region, aid for those who are persecuted by courts or the police (*gamonales* prosecute Indigenous peoples who resist them or whose lands they wish to take), defense of communal property, and the organization of small libraries and study centers.

In Peru, the organization and education of the mining proletariat is, together with that of the agricultural proletariat, one of the most pressing issues. The mining centers, the largest of which (La Oroya) is on the way to becoming the most important profit center in South America, constitute points where class propaganda can advantageously operate. Apart from representing themselves in substantial proletarian concentrations with the conditions similar to wage owners, Indigenous day laborers work alongside industrial workers who bring the class spirit and principles to those centers. The Indigenous people of the mines, to a large extent, continue to be peasants, so that the adherents won among them are also elements won among the peasant class.

This work, in all its aspects, will be difficult. But its progress will fundamentally depend on the ability of the activists who carry it out, and their precise and concrete appreciation of the objective conditions of the Indigenous question. The problem is not racial but rather social and economic. But race has a role in it and in the means of confronting it. For example, only militants from the Indigenous milieu can, because of their mentality and language, achieve an effective and immediate influence over their comrades.

A revolutionary Indigenous consciousness will perhaps take time to form, but once Indians have made the socialist idea their own, they will serve it with a discipline, a tenacity, and a strength, that few other proletarians of other milieus will be able to surpass.

The reality of grounded and precise revolutionary politics in which the appreciation and utilization of the circumstances on which one must act in countries where the Indigenous or Black population has an important size and role can and must turn the factor of race into a revolutionary factor. It is essential to give the movement of the Indigenous and Black proletariat, whether agricultural or industrial, a clear character of class struggle. "One must give Indigenous or enslaved Black populations," said a Brazilian comrade, "the certainty that only a government of workers and peasants of all races who inhabit the territory will truly emancipate them, since only that will terminate the rule of large estate owners and the industrial capitalist system, and definitively liberate them from imperialist oppression."

Bourgeois Colonial and Imperialist Policy Concerning the Races[13]

To carry out intense exploitation, the colonial powers have sought a series of legal and religious pretexts to legitimize their attitude, starting from the concept of racial "inferiority."

Too well-known is the thesis of Pope Alexander VI, who, as a representative of God on Earth, divided among the Catholic kings of Spain and Portugal, the power over Latin America, on the condition that they become the tutors of the Indigenous race. These Indigenous people, as "idolaters," could not enjoy the same rights as the loyal subjects of the Catholic majesties. On the other hand, it was not possible to sanction "*by law*" the anti-Christian formula of slavery. The hypocritical formula of guardianship then emerged with one of its most representative economic expressions—the "*encomienda*." The fittest Spaniards were elected "*encomenderos*" from different territories that comprised a large Indian population. Their mission was twofold. In the spiritual order, they should convert the Indians to the Catholic faith; the means of persuasion were provided whenever necessary, by the *doctrineros*. In the temporal order, the task was even simpler; each "encomienda" should provide the crown with a corresponding tribute, notwithstanding that the *encomendero* will also take out the amount he deems appropriate. Later we will see the specific characteristics of the "encomiendas" and the process by which they constituted a legal method of plundering the lands of the natives, laying the foundations of the colonial and semi-feudal property that subsists until today.

In this process, it is necessary to underline here an important factor in the submission of aboriginal populations to the economic and political power of the invaders. The invading race that appeared protected by almost invulnerable armor, mounted marvelously on unknown animals, the horses, fighting with weapons that threw fire; this race that demolished in a few decades and then quickly subdued an immense empire like the Inca and numerous jungle tribes such as those of Brazil, Uruguay, and Paraguay, logically had a great ascendency to impose their gods and their cult on the ruins of the Incan temples, on the defeated myths of the religion of the sun and the anthropomorphic fetishism of other Indians.

The invaders did not neglect the loss of prestige they had brought upon the the cross with their weapons and quickly proceeded to enchain the souls all the while enslaving the bodies. This greatly facilitated economic submission, the primordial object of the Catholic minions. In this process, it is interesting to note the results obtained by the invaders. Wherever a blind and brutal domination decimated Aboriginal people in alarming ways for the sake of production, the yield of production declined to the point of requiring the importation of the African race, especially for the work of the mines. However, the newly imported slaves were often ill-equipped for that sort of work.

Where the penetration of the land was carried out more shrewdly and fostered under the determined protection of the Crown, they looked to take possession of consciences. The Catholic missions managed to establish flourishing plantations even in the heart of the jungles where, if the Indian did not cease to be exploited, production and the amount of benefits to the invaders increased progressively. The historical examples of the Jesuit colonies in Brazil and Paraguay, as well as the colonies that other religious congregations established in the jungles of Peru, are quite demonstrative in this regard. Today, the influence of religion is still an important factor in the submission of the Indians to the civil and religious "authorities." The difference being that, in their heightened idiocy, these authorities have taken to the land this shameless robbery carried out by corporal punishment and are taking part in the most shameful of business practices, thereby managing to create a feeling of revulsion for the priest, as well as for the judge, a feeling that is becoming more evident every day and has burst more than once into bloody revolt.

A large sector of the priests, allied to the national bourgeoisie, continues to use their weapons, based on religious fanaticism, that several centuries of propaganda have managed to ingrain in the consciousness of the Indians. Only class consciousness, only the revolutionary "myth" with its deep economic roots, and not an infectious anti-clerical propaganda, will be able to replace the artificial myths imposed by the "civilization" of the invaders and maintained by the bourgeois classes—the heirs of their power.

Imperialists have also attempted to build a more resilient and pervasive base in Latin America for their ominous power. The Methodist and Anglican missions and the moralizing sports centers of the YMCA have even managed to penetrate the mountains of Peru and Bolivia, but with absolutely negligible success and without the possibility of extending their action. A fierce adversary to such penetration was found in the village priest, who saw the danger of diminishing his spiritual influence and the consequent pecuniary revenues. There were cases in which the village priest managed to obtain the support of the civil authorities and definitively banish the "anti-Catholic" Protestant missions.

Other factors linked to the social nature of the exploited have been employed by the colony and continued by a large sector of the bourgeoisie and imperialists. The contempt for the Indian and the black has been inoculated by the white, by all means, to the mestizo. It is not uncommon to notice this same attitude in mestizos whose Indian origin is too obvious and whose percentage of white blood becomes difficult to recognize. This contempt that has been fostered within the working-class, grows considerably as the mestizo occupies higher degrees with respect to the last layers of the exploited proletariat, without thereby diminishing the deep barrier that separates them from the white population.

For the same purposes, the feudalist and bourgeoisie have fed a deep feeling of animosity for Indians to Black people, facilitated, as we have already said, by the role that the latter filled in countries with small Indian populations: craftsmen, domestic servants, watchmen, always next to the bosses, enjoying a certain familiarity that gave them the "right" to despise everything their employers despised.

The exploiters have also never neglected the opportunity to create rivalries between groups of the same race. American imperialism gives us a concrete example of this tactic in the rivalry that it managed to create between Blacks residing in Cuba and those who periodically come from Haiti and Jamaica to work, impelled by the harsh conditions of their country of origin.

Nor have some intellectual sectors identified with the bourgeoisie ceased to seek more weapons to denigrate the Indians until they deny truthfulness to the most salient characters of their historical process.

Authors dedicated to writing pseudo-historical works assert that one cannot talk about community structures among the Inca Indians. These people, of course, intended to close their eyes to the existence of thousands of communities in Peru, Bolivia, and Chile, where millions of Indians still live after the collapse of their public order, three centuries of colonization, and a century of bourgeois and ecclesiastical feudal pillage. The task of pulverizing these absurd theses, largely consisting of the same bourgeois criticism, will be taken over by the nascent Marxist critique of this problem, whose historical studies we already have bright signs of in Latin America.

Later on, I will detail the main characteristics that the primitive collectivism had and has in the Indians.

What is more, it is my duty to point out that one of the most urgent tasks of our parties is the immediate revision of all the histories accumulated by the feudal and bourgeois critics, which is elaborated to their benefit by the Department of Statistics of the capitalist states and offered for our consideration in all its deformity, thereby impeding our understanding of the values of the aboriginal races.

Only knowledge of concrete reality, acquired through work and the development of all Communist parties, can enable us to draw directives based off of existing conditions. Our historical research is useful, but most of all we must control the current state and sentiment, probe the orientation of its collective thinking, evaluate its forces of expansion and resistance. All this, we know, is conditioned by historical background, on the one hand, but, mainly, by its current economic conditions. We should understand these conditions in all their detail. The life of the Indian, the conditions of their exploitation, the possibilities of struggle on their part, the most practical means of immersing the proletariat vanguard among them, the most apt way in which they can constitute their organization; here are the fundamental points, whose knowledge we must pursue to accurately fill the historical task that each party must carry out.

The class struggle—a fundamental reality that our parties recognize—undoubtedly has special characteristics when the vast majority of the exploited are constituted by one race, and the exploiters belong almost exclusively to another.

I have tried to demonstrate some of the essentially racial problems that capitalism and imperialism deepen as well as some of the weaknesses, due to the cultural deprivation of the races, that capitalism exploits to its exclusive benefit.

The hardest economic oppression weighs on the shoulders of the producing class and is compounded by racial contempt and hatred. A simple and clear understanding of such situations is needed so that this mass may rise as one being and throw off all forms of exploitation.

Source: *Ideología y Política*

5

PROGRAMMATIC PRINCIPLES OF THE SOCIALIST PARTY

The program should be a doctrinal statement that affirms:

1. The international character of the contemporary economy, which does not allow any country to avoid the currents of transformation arising from the current conditions of production.

2. The international character of the revolutionary proletarian movement. The Socialist Party adapts its praxis to the specific circumstances of the country, but it obeys a broad class vision, and the same national circumstances are subordinated to the rhythm of world history. The independence revolution more than a century ago was a movement in solidarity with all peoples subjugated by Spain; the socialist revolution is a joint movement of all peoples oppressed by capitalism. If the liberal revolution, nationalist in principle, could not be achieved without a close union between the South American countries, it is easy to understand the historical law imposes that the social revolution, internationalist in its principles, operate with a much more disciplined and intense coordination of proletarian parties in an era of more pronounced interdependence and linking of nations. The manifesto of Marx and Engels condenses the first principle of the proletarian revolution in the historical phrase: "Workers of the world, unite!"

3. The sharpening of the contradictions in the capitalist economy. Capitalism has emerged in a semi-feudal context such as ours, at the stage of monopolies and imperialism, when free competition no longer corresponds to liberal ideology. Imperialism does not consent to any of these semi-colonial peoples, which operates as a market for its capital and merchandise and as a deposit of raw materials, an economic program of nationalization and industrialism. It forces them to specialization, to monoculture. (Oil, copper, sugar, cotton, in Peru.) Crises derive from this rigid determination of national production by factors of the capitalist world market.

4. Capitalism is in its imperialist stage. It is the capitalism of monopolies, of finance capital, of imperialist wars for the plundering of markets and sources of raw materials. The practice of Marxist socialism in this period is that of Marxism-Leninism. Marxism-Leninism is the revolutionary method in the stage of imperialism and monopolies. The Peruvian Socialist Party adopts it as its method of struggle.

5. The pre-capitalist economy of republican Peru that, due to the absence of a strong bourgeois class and the national and international conditions that have caused the country's slow progress along the capitalist road, cannot be liberated under a bourgeois regime subjected to imperialist interests. It colludes with *gamonalist* and clerical feudality, and suffers from the defects and vestiges of colonial feudalism.

The colonial fate of the country determines its process. The emancipation of the country's economy is possible only by the action of the proletarian masses in solidarity with the global anti-imperialist struggle. Only proletarian action can first stimulate and then carry out the tasks of the bourgeois-democratic revolution, which the bourgeois regime is incapable of developing and delivering.

6. Socialism finds the same elements of a solution to the land question in the livelihoods of communities as it does in large agricultural enterprises. In areas where the presence of the *yanaconazgo* sharecropping system or small landholdings require keeping individual management, the solution will be the partial exploitation of the land by small farmers, while at the same time moving toward the collective management of agriculture in areas where this type of exploitation prevails. But this, like the stimulation that freely provides for the resurgence of Indigenous peoples, the creative manifestation of their forces and native spirit, does not mean at all a romantic and anti-historical trend of reconstructing or resurrecting Inca social-ism, which corresponded to historical conditions completely bypassed, and which remains only as a fa-vorable factor in a perfectly scientific production technique, that is, the habits of cooperation and so-cialism of Indigenous peasants. Socialism presuppos-es the technology, science, and capitalist stage. It can-not permit any setbacks in the realization of the achievements of modern civilization, but on the con-trary, it must methodically accelerate the incorpora-tion of these achievements into national life.

7. Only socialism can solve the problem of an effec-tively democratic and egalitarian education, by virtue of which each member of society receives all the in-struction to which his capacity entitles him. The so-cialist educational regime is the only one that can fully and systematically apply the principles of the school system, of technical school, of school communities, and in general of all the ideals of contemporary revo-lutionary pedagogy. These are incompatible with the privileges of the capitalist school, which condemns the poor classes to cultural inferiority and makes higher education the monopoly of the wealthy.

8. Passing its bourgeois-democratic stage, the revolu-tion becomes in its objectives and its doctrine a prole-tarian revolution. The proletarian party, trained by the struggle for the control of power and the develop-ment of its own program, performs at this stage the tasks of organizing and defending the socialist order.

9. The Peruvian Socialist Party is the vanguard of the proletariat, the political force that assumes the task of guiding and leading the struggle for the realization of its class ideals.

Immediate Demands

• Broad recognition of freedom of association, assembly, and press.

• Recognition of the right of all workers to strike.

• Abolition of roadwork conscription.

• Replacement of the vagrancy law with articles that specifically considered the issue of vagrancy in the preliminary draft of the Criminal Code enacted by the State, with the sole exception of those articles that are incompatible with the spirit and criminal criteria of the special law.

• Establishment of state-funded Social Security and State Social Assistance

• Compliance with the laws of worker's compensation, protection of the rights of working women and children, and protection for the eight-hour day in agricultural work.

• Add malaria in the coastal valleys to the list of work-related diseases that landowners are responsible for treating.

• Establishment of the seven-hour day in the mines and in places that are unhealthy, dangerous, and harmful to the worker's health.

• The requirement of mining and oil companies to permanently and effectively recognize all the rights of workers that are guaranteed by the laws of the country.

• Increase in wages in industry, agriculture, mining, sea and land transport, and the guano islands, in proportion to the cost of living and the right of workers to a higher standard of living.

• Complete abolition of all forced or unpaid labor. Abolish or penalize of the semi-slave regime in the montaña region.

• Break up lands belonging to the large *latifundia* and distribute them among the estates' workers in sufficient proportion to their needs.

• Expropriation, without compensation, of all the estates belonging to convents and religious congregations in order to give them to rural communities.

• Obtain legal rights for the *yanacono* sharecroppers, tenants, etc., who work a land more than three consecutive years, to continue to use the plots through annual rents not exceeding 60 percent of the current lease fee. Discount at least 50 percent of this fee for all those who continue as sharecroppers or tenants.

• Award cooperatives and poor peasants with land put into agricultural production through irrigation projects.

• Maintain everywhere the rights granted to employees by the law. Regulate pension rights with a parity commission that does not result in the slightest reduction of those rights as established by law.

• Introduce a minimum wage and salary.

• Ratification of freedom of religion and religious education, at least in the terms of the constitutional article, and consequent repeal of the last decree against non-Catholic schools.

• Make education free at all levels.

The very act of the public establishment of this groups lays claim to the rights of the freedom for the party to act lawfully and openly under the Constitution and to claim the guarantees it grants to citizens to access press freedoms without restrictions and to hold congress and debates. Closely associated groups to those that today address the public through this statement resolutely assume, through the consciousness of a duty and an historic responsibility, the mission to defend and propagate its principles and to maintain and enhance its organization, at the expense of any sacrifice. And the working masses of the city, the countryside, the mining camps, and Indigenous peasants, whose interests and aspirations we represent in the political struggle, will embrace these claims and ideas, will fight persistently and vigorously for them, and will find, through each struggle, the road that leads to the final victory of socialism.

Source: *Ideología y Política*

6

ANTI-IMPERIALIST POINT OF VIEW

I

To what extent can the situation of the Latin American republics be compared to that of other semi-colonial countries? The economic condition of these republics is undoubtedly semi-colonial, and, as their capitalism and, consequently, imperialist penetration, grows, this character of their economy is accentuated. But the national bourgeoisie, who see cooperation with imperialism as the best source of benefits, feel they are sufficiently in possession of political power to not worry seriously about national sovereignty. The South American bourgeoisie who still do not know, with the exception of Panama, Yankee military occupation, have no predisposition to accept the need to fight for a second independence, as the APRA[1] propaganda naively assumed. The State, or rather the ruling class, does not feel the need for a broader and more certain degree of national autonomy. The Revolution of Independence is relatively too close, its myths and symbols too alive in the consciousness of the bourgeoisie and the petite-bourgeoisie. The illusion of national sovereignty remains intact. It would be a serious error to assume that this social layer retains a sense of revolutionary nationalism that in other conditions would represent a factor of the anti-imperialist struggle in semi-colonial countries overwhelmed by imperialism as in Asia in recent decades.

Over a year ago in our discussion with the leaders of the APRA, we rejected their desire to create a Latin American Kuomintang, and as a way to avoid imitating Europe and to accommodate revolutionary action to a precise assessment of our own reality, we put forward the following thesis:

Collaboration with the bourgeoisie, and even of many feudal elements, in the Chinese anti-imperialist struggle, is explained on the grounds of race and national civilization that do not exist for us. The Chinese nobility or bourgeoisie feels intimately Chinese. They respond to white contempt for their stratified and decrepit culture with the contempt and pride of their ancient traditions. Anti-imperialism in China may, therefore, rest on sentiments and the nationalist factor. In Indo-America, the circumstances are not the same. The Creole aristocracy and bourgeoisie do not feel a sense of solidarity with the people through the bond of a common history and culture. In Peru, the white aristocrats and bourgeoisie despise the popular and national elements. They are, above all, whites. The petit-bourgeois mestizo imitates this example. Lima's bourgeoisie fraternizes with the Yankee capitalists, and even with their mere employees, in the country clubs, in the tennis courts, and in the streets: the Yankee marries the elite creole girl without any inconvenience of race or religion, and she in turn does not feel a scruple of nationality or culture in preferring to marry an individual of the invading race. Nor does the middle class girl have this scruple. The *"huachafita"*[2] that can catch a Yankee employee of Grace Company or the Rockefeller Foundation does so with the satisfaction of those who feel their social status rise. The nationalist factor, for these objective reasons that none of you can escape, is not decisive or fundamental in the anti-imperialist struggle in our context. Only in countries like Argentina, where there is a large and rich bourgeoisie proud of their country's wealth and power, and where the national character has for these reasons clear and more precise characteristics than in more backward countries, could anti-imperialism (perhaps) penetrate easily into the bourgeoisie. But this is for reasons of capitalist expansion and growth and not for reasons of social justice and socialist doctrine as is our case.

The betrayal of the Chinese bourgeoisie and the failure of the Kuomintang was not yet known in all its magnitude. Their capitalist style of nationalism (one not related to social justice or theory) demonstrates how little one can trust the revolutionary nationalist sentiments of the bourgeoisie, even in countries like China.

As long as the imperialist policy manages the feelings and formalities of the national sovereignty of these states, as long as it is not forced to resort to armed intervention and military occupation, it will absolutely count on the collaboration of the bourgeoisie. Although dominated by the imperialist economy, these countries, or rather their bourgeoisie, will consider themselves masters of their own destinies, as do Romania, Bulgaria, Poland, and other "dependent" countries of Europe.

This factor of political psychology should not be neglected in estimating the possibilities of anti-imperialist action in Latin America. Its relegation, its forgetfulness, has been one of the characteristics of APRA's theory.

II

The fundamental difference between the elements in Peru that accepted the APRA in principle—as a united front plan, but never as a party and not even as an effective ongoing organization—and those outside Peru that later defined it as a Latin American Kuomintang, is that the former remain faithful to the revolutionary socioeconomic conception of anti-imperialism, while the latter explain their position by saying: "We are leftists (or socialists) because we are anti-imperialists." Anti-imperialism is thus elevated to the category of a program, of a political attitude, of a movement that is self-sufficient and that leads, spontaneously, though we do not know by virtue of what process, to socialism, to the social revolution. This concept leads to an exorbitant overestimation of the anti-imperialist movement, to the exaggeration of the myth of the struggle for the "second independence," and romanticizes that we are already living in the days of a new emancipation. The result is the tendency to replace anti-imperialist leagues with the political party. Initially conceived as a united front, as a popular alliance, as a block of the oppressed classes, APRA has come to be defined as the Latin American Kuomintang.

For us, anti-imperialism does not and cannot constitute, by itself, a political program, a mass movement capable of fully seizing power. Anti-imperialism, even if it could mobilize the bourgeoisie and petite-bourgeoisie alongside the working-class and peasant masses (we have already discounted this possibility), does not nullify antagonisms between classes, nor does it suppress different class interests.

Neither the bourgeoisie nor the petite-bourgeoisie in power can pursue anti-imperialist policies. We have the experience of Mexico, where the petite bourgeoisie has come to an agreement with Yankee imperialism. A "nationalist" government may use, in its relations with the United States, a different language than the Leguía government in Peru. This government is, frankly, uninhibitedly pan-Americanist and Monroist, but any other bourgeois government would do practically the same thing in terms of loans and concessions. Investments of foreign capital in Peru grow in a close and direct relationship with the county's economic development, with the exploitation of its natural wealth, with the population of its territory, with the increase in routes of communication. How can the most demagogic petite bourgeoisie oppose capitalist penetration? With nothing but words. Nothing but a temporary nationalist drunkenness.

The taking of power by anti-imperialism as a populist demagogic movement, if possible, would not represent the conquest of power by the proletarian masses or by socialism. The socialist revolution would find its most fierce and dangerous enemy—dangerous for its confusion and demagogy—in the petite-bourgeoisie put in power by voices of order.

Without eliminating the use of any type of anti-imperialist agitation, nor any means of mobilization of the social sectors that may eventually contribute to this struggle, our mission is to explain and demonstrate to the masses that only the socialist revolution will oppose the advance of imperialism—a definitive and true fence.

III

These facts differentiate the situation of the South American countries from the situation of the Central American countries, where Yankee imperialism, resorting to armed intervention without any qualms, provokes a patriotic reaction that can easily win over a part of the bourgeoisie and petite bourgeoisie to anti-imperialism. The APRA propaganda, personally conducted by Haya de la Torre, does not seem to have obtained anywhere else in America greater results. His confusing and messianic sermons, which although they intend to place themselves at the level of the economic struggle, actually appeal in particular to racial and sentimental factors, thereby meeting the conditions necessary to impress the petit-bourgeois intellectuals. The formation of class parties and powerful trade union organizations, with a clear class consciousness, does not appear destined in those countries for the same immediate development as in South America. In our countries, the class factor is more decisive, it is more developed. There is no reason to resort to vague populist formulas after which reactionary tendencies can only thrive. At the moment the *aprismo*, like propaganda, is circumscribed to Central America; in South America, as a result of the populist, *caudillista*, petite-bourgeois deviation, which defined it as the Latin American Kuomintang, it is in a stage of total liquidation. Whatever the next Anti-Imperialist Congress in Paris resolves, its decisions must decide on the unification of anti-imperialist organizations and to distinguish between anti-imperialist platforms and agitation and the tasks that fall within the competence of working-class parties and trade union organizations. It will have the final say on the issue.

IV

Do the interests of imperialist capitalism necessarily and inevitably coincide with the feudal and semi-feudal interests of our countries' landowning classes? Is the struggle against feudalism unavoidably and completely identical with the anti-imperialist struggle? Certainly, imperialist capitalism uses the power of the feudal class to the degree that it considers it the

politically dominant class. But their economic interests are not the same. The petite-bourgeoisie, even
the most demagogic, can end up in the same intimate
alliance with imperialist capitalism if it, in practice,
dilutes its most conspicuous nationalist impulses. Finance capital would feel more secure if power were in
the hands of a larger social class that is in a better position than the old, hated feudal class to defend the interests of capitalism and serve as its guard and water
boy by satisfying certain overdue demands and dis-
torting the masses' class orientation. The creation of a
class of smallholders, the expropriation of the latifundia, and the liquidation of feudal privileges are not in
opposition to the interests of imperialism in an immediate sense. On the contrary, to the degree that feudal
vestiges still remain despite the growth of the capitalist economy, the movement for the liquidation of feudal privileges coincides with the interests of capitalist
development as promoted by imperialist experts and
investments. The disappearance of the large *latifundia*, the creation of an agrarian economy through what
bourgeois demagoguery calls the "democratization"
of the land, the displacement of the old aristocracies
by a more powerful bourgeoisie and petite-bourgeoisie better able to guarantee social peace—none of
this is contrary to imperialist interests. The Leguia
regime in Peru, as timid as it has been in regard to the
interests of the *latifundistas* and *gamonales* (who support it to a great degree), has no problem resorting to
demagogy, declaiming against feudalism and feudal
privilege, thundering against the old oligarchies, and
promoting a program of land distribution to make every field worker a small landowner. The Leguía
regime draws its greatest strength from precisely this

type of demagogy. The Leguía regime does not dare lay a hand on the large landowners. But the natural direction of capitalist development—irrigation works, the exploitation of new mines, etc.—is in contradiction to the interests and privileges of feudalism. To the degree that the amount of cultivated land increases and new centers of employment appear, the *latifundistas* lose their principal power: the absolute and unconditional control of labor. In Lambayeque, where a water diversion project has been started by the American engineer Sutton, the technical commission has already run up against the interests of the large feudal landowners. These landowners grow mainly sugar. The threat that they will lose their monopoly of land and water, and thereby their means of controlling the work force, infuriates these people and pushes them toward attitudes that the government considers subversive, no matter how closely it is connected to these elements. Sutton has all the characteristics of the North American capitalist businessman. His outlook and his work clash with the feudal spirit of the *latifundistas*. For example, Sutton has established a system of water distribution that is based on the principle that these resources belong to the state; the *latifundistas* believe that water rights are part of their right to the land. By this theory, the water was theirs: it was and is the absolute property of their estates.

V

And is the petite-bourgeoisie, whose role in the struggle against imperialism is so often overestimated, necessarily opposed to imperialist penetration because of its economic exploitation? The petite-bourgeoisie is undoubtedly the social class most sensitive to the fascination of nationalist mythology. But the economic factor which predominates is the following: in countries afflicted with Spanish-style poverty, where the petite-bourgeoisie, locked in decades-old prejudice, resists proletarianization; where, because of their miserable wages, they do not have the economic power to partially transform themselves into a working class; where the desperate search for office employment, a petty government job, and the hunt for a "decent" salary and a "decent" job dominate, the creation of large enterprises that represent better-paid jobs, even if they enormously exploit their local employees, is favorably received by the middle classes. A Yankee business represents a better salary, possibilities for advancement, and liberation from dependence on the state, which can only offer a future to speculators. This reality acts with a decisive force on the consciousness of the petit-bourgeois searching for or having found a job. In these countries with Spanish-style poverty, we repeat, the situation of the middle classes is not the same as in those countries where these classes have gone through a period of free competition and of capitalist growth favorable to individual initiative and success and to the oppression of large monopolies.

In conclusion, we are anti-imperialists because we are Marxists, because we are revolutionaries, because we oppose capitalism with socialism as an adversarial system called to succeed it. In the fight against foreign imperialism, we fulfill our duties of solidarity with the revolutionary masses of Europe.

Source: *Ideología y Política*

7

NATIONALISM AND VANGUARDISM

In Political Ideology

I

The sensibility of the new generation is the most Peruvian, the most national of contemporary Peru. This assertion will possibly amuse some recalcitrant yet sincere conservatives. It is, however, one of the easiest truths to prove. The fact that conservatives do not and cannot understand this is something that is perfectly explicable. But that does not diminish nor obscure the evidence.

To understand how the new generation feels and thinks, a faithful and serious critic would undoubtedly begin by finding out its demands. They would have to verify, therefore, that the primary demand of our vanguard is the demand of the Indian. This fact does not tolerate mystification or misinterpretation.

Translated into an intelligible language for all, including conservatives, the Indigenous problem presents itself as the problem of four million Peruvians. Explained in nationalist terms, it is the problem of assimilation of four fifths of the population of Peru into the Peruvian nation.

How can one deny the Peruvianness of an ideology and of a program that proclaims its yearning and its willingness to solve this problem with such vehement burning?

II

The disciples of the monarchist nationalism of *L'Action Française* likely adopt the formula of Maurras: "All that is national is ours." But these conservatives are very careful in defining the national, the Peruvian. Theoretically and practically, the conservative *criollo* behaves as an heir to the colony and as a descendant of conquest. For pasadistas,[1] the national begins in the colonial. The Indigenous are in their sentiment, but not in their thesis. They are regarded as strictly pre-national. Conservatism can only conceive of or admit a Peruvian formed in the molds of Spain and Rome. This sense of Peruvianness has serious consequences for the theory and practice of that nationalism which it inspires and breeds. The first is that it limits the history of the Peruvian homeland to four centuries. And four centuries of tradition must seem very little to any nationalism, even the most modest and illusory. No solid nationalism appears in our time as an elaboration of only four centuries of history.

To feel a more respectable and illustrious antiquity behind them, reactionary nationalists invariably resort to the artifice of annexing not only the whole past and all the glory of Spain but also the whole past and the glory of *latinidad*. According to them, the roots of nationality are Spanish and Latin. Peru, as these people represent it, does not descend from the native Inca; it descends from the foreign empire that imposed its law, religion, and language four centuries ago.

Maurice Barrés, in a phrase that is certainly held as an article of faith by our reactionaries, said that the homeland is the land and its dead. No nationalism can do without land. This is the drama that, in addition to availing itself of an imported ideology, represents the spirit and interests of the conquest and the colony in Peru.

III

In opposition to this spirit, the vanguard advocates Peruvian reconstruction on an Indigenous foundation. The new generation is reclaiming our true past, our true history. Among us, *pasadistas* are satisfied with the fragile gallant memories of the viceroyalty. The vanguard, meanwhile, seeks for its work more genuinely Peruvian, more remotely ancient, materials.

And their *Indigenismo* is not a literary speculation

or a romantic pastime. It is not an *Indigenismo* that, like many others, is resolved and exhausted in an innocuous apology of the Inca Empire and its splendors. The revolutionary *indigenistas*, instead of a platonic love for the Inca past, manifest an active and concrete solidarity with today's Indian.

This *Indigenismo* does not indulge in fantasies of utopian restorations. It sees the past as a foundation, not a program. This conception of historic events is realistic and modern. It does not ignore or forget any of the historical facts that have modified the world's reality, as well as Peru's, in these four centuries.

IV

It is supposed that when young people are seduced by foreign perspectives and exotic doctrines, they are probably based on a superficial interpretation of the relations between nationalism and socialism. Socialism is not, in any country in the world, an anti-national movement. It may seem so, perhaps, in empires. In England, in France, in the United States, etc., the revolutionaries denounce and fight the imperialism of their own governments. But the function of the socialist idea changes in politically or economically colonial peoples. In these villages, socialism acquires, by force of circumstance, without denying entirely any of its principles, a nationalist attitude. Those who follow the process of Moroccan, Egyptian, Chinese, or Indian nationalist agitation can easily explain this totally logical aspect of revolutionary praxis. They observe, from the outset, the essentially popular character of such agitation. Western imperialism and capitalism always encounter minimal resistance, if not complete submission, in conservative classes and the dominant castes of colonial peoples. The demands for national independence receive their momentum and their energy from the popular masses. In Turkey, where the most vigorous and auspicious nationalist movement has operated in recent years, this phenomenon can fully and accurately studied. Turkey has been reborn as a nation on the merit and work of its revolutionary people, not its conservatives. The same historical impulse that drove the Greeks out of Asia Minor and inflicted a defeat on British imperialism, drove the caliph and his court out of Constantinople.

One of the most interesting phenomena, one of the most extensive movements of this era, is precisely this revolutionary nationalism, this revolutionary patriotism. As an internationalist has said, the idea of the nation is, in certain historical periods, the embodiment of the spirit of freedom. In the Western Europe, where it is now most dated, it began and developed as a revolutionary idea. It now has this value for all peoples fighting against imperialist exploitation for their national freedom.

In Peru, those who represent and interpret Peruvianness as an affirmation and not as a denial work to give a homeland to those who, having been conquered and subdued by the Spaniards, lost it four centuries ago and have not yet recovered it.

In Literature and Art

I

Those who have no wish to venture into other fields will easily see the national sense and value of all positive and authentic vanguardism in literature and art. The most national of any literature is always the most profoundly revolutionary. This is very logical and clear.

A new school, a new literary or artistic tendency seeks its foundation in the present. If it does not find this, it perishes. On the other hand, the old schools, the old tendencies, are content to represent the spiritual and formal remnants of the past.

Therefore, conceiving the nation as a static reality can only be imagined as a national spirit and inspiration among the imitators and enthusiasts of an old art, and not by the creators or innovators of a new art. A nation lives more so in the precursors of its future than in the survivors of its past.

II

I have already had the occasion to argue that the Italian Futurist movement cannot be recognized as anything other than a spontaneous gesture of Italy's genius, and that the iconoclasts who proposed to cleanse Italy of its museums, ruins, relics, and all its venerable objects were deeply moved by a profound love for Italy.

The study of the biology of Italian Futurism inevitably leads to this conclusion. Futurism represented a moment of Italian consciousness, not as a literary and artistic mode, but as a spiritual attitude. Futurist artists and writers, rising loudly and harshly against the vestiges of the past, affirmed Italy's right and aptitude to renew itself and surpass itself in literature and art.

Having accomplished this mission, Futurism ceased to be a movement supported by the purest and highest artistic values of Italy, as it was in its early days. But the mood it had aroused has persisted. And the fascist phenomenon, whose roots are so purely national according to its apologists, was in part prepared by this emotional state. Futurism became fascist because art does not dominate politics, and, above all, because it was the fascists who conquered Rome. But it would just as easily would have become socialist if the proletarian revolution had been victoriously carried out. And in this case, its luck would have been different. Instead of disappearing permanently as an art movement or school (as has been its fate under fascism), Futurism would then have seen a dynamic revival. Fascism, after having exploited its impulse and spirit, has forced Futurism to accept its reactionary principles, that is, to repudiate itself theoretically and practically. The revolution, meanwhile, would have stimulated and increased the will to create a new art in a new society.

This has been the fate of Futurism in Russia, for example. Russian Futurism had been more or less a twin of Italian Futurist movement. Continuous and intimate relations existed between both futurisms. And just as Italian Futurism followed fascism, so Russian Futurism joined the proletarian revolution. Russia is the only country in Europe where Futurism has been elevated to the category of official art, as Guillermo de Torre has noted with satisfaction.

In Russia, this victory has not been obtained at the cost of renunciation. Futurism in Russia has continued to be Futurism. It has not been tamed as in Italy. It has continued to see itself as an agent of the future. While Italian Futurism no longer has a single great poet in full command of their iconoclastic and futurist belligerence, in Russia Mayakovsky, the troubadour of the revolution, has achieved the most enduring triumphs in this craft.

III

But to more exactly and precisely establish the national character of all vanguardism, let us return to our America. The new poets of Argentina are an interesting example. All of them are nurtured by European aesthetics. All, or almost all, have traveled in one of those wagons of the Grand European Express which for Blaise Centrars, Valery Larbaud and Paul Morand are undoubtedly the vehicles of European unity as well as indispensable elements of a new literary sensibility.

And this is fine. Despite the impregnation of cosmopolitanism, despite their ecumenical conception of art, the best of these vanguard poets are still the most Argentine. The Argentineanness of Girondo, Güiraldes, Borges, etc. is no less evident than their cosmopolitanism. The Argentine literary avant-garde is called "Fierrismo." Anyone who has ever read *Martín Fierro*, the periodical of this nucleus of artists, will have found in it the most authentic Gaucho elements alongside the most recent echoes of Europe's ultra-modern art.

What is the secret of this ability to feel both international and national events? The answer is simple. The personality of the artist, the human personality, is only fully realized when it ascends all limitations.

IV

We observe the same phenomenon in Peruvian literature, although with less intensity. While Peruvian literature retained a conservative and academic character, it could not be truly and profoundly Peruvian. Until a few years ago, our literature has been only a modest colony of Spanish literature. Its transformation in this respect, as in others, began with the *"Colónida"* movement. The case of Valdelomar is one in which cosmopolitan and national sentiment come together and combine. The snobbish love of European fashions did not stifle or attenuate Valdelomar's love of the rustic and humble things of his own land and village. On the contrary, it perhaps contributed to arousing and exalting it within him.

And now the phenomenon is accentuated. What perhaps attracts and excites us the most in the Poet César Vallejo is the indigenous foundation, the autochthonous background of his art. Vallejo is quite indigenous, and he is very much ours. The fact that we esteem and understand him is not a product of chance. Nor is it an exclusive consequence of his genius. Rather, it is proof that, through these cosmopolitan and ecumenical journeys for which we are so reproached, we are increasingly discovering ourselves.

Source: *Peruanicemos al Perú*

8

HETERODOXY OF TRADITION

I have written at the end of my article "Reivindi-
cación de Jorge Manrique" (The claim of Jorge Manrique):

> His poetry has do with tradition, but not the traditional-
> ists. Because tradition is, contrary to what the tradition-
> alists want, alive and dynamic. Those who deny tradi-
> tion create it to renew and enrich it. Those who want
> tradition dead and static kill it, extending parts of the
> past into a powerless present to incorporate their spirit
> and blood into it.[1]

These words deserve to be earnestly stressed and
explained. Since I have written them, I feel invited to
release a revolutionary thesis of tradition. I am speaking, of course, of tradition understood as heritage and
historical continuity.

Is it true that revolutionaries deny it and repudiate

it en bloc? This is what those who are content with the gratuitous formula want: iconoclastic revolutionaries. But are revolutionaries nothing more than iconoclasts? When Marinetti invited Italy to sell its museums and monuments, he wanted only to affirm the creative power of his homeland, too oppressed by the weight of an overwhelmingly glorious past. It would have been absurd to take his vehement extremism at face value. All revolutionary doctrine acts on reality by means of intransigent denials that cannot be understood except by interpreting them in their dialectical role.

True revolutionaries never act as if history begins with them. They know that they represent historical forces whose existence does not allow them to indulge in the ultraistic fable of inaugurating all things. Marx drew from the complete study of bourgeois economics his principles of socialist politics. All the industrial and financial experience of capitalism is in his anti-capitalist doctrine. Proudhon, of whom everyone knows the iconoclastic phrase, but not the long-winded work, cemented his ideals in an arduous analysis of social institutions and customs, examining from their roots to the soil and the air from which they were nurtured. And Sorel, in whom Marx and Proudhon reconcile, was deeply concerned not only with the formation of the legal consciousness of the proletariat, but with the influence of family organization and its moral stimuli, both in the means of production and in the entire social equilibrium.

Tradition should not be identified with traditionalists. Traditionalism—not in the sense of a philosophical doctrine, but a political or sentimental attitude that invariably resolves itself into mere conservatism —is truly the greatest enemy of tradition. This is because it is obstinately focused on defining tradition as a set of inert relics and extinct symbols, and to summarize it in a concise and particular recipe.

Tradition, meanwhile, is characterized precisely by its resistance to being apprehended in a hermetic formula. As a result of a series of experiences—that is, of successive transformations of reality under the action of an ideal that surpasses it by consulting it and models it by obeying it—the tradition is heterogeneous and contradictory in its components. To reduce it to a single concept, it is to be content with its essence, thereby renouncing its various crystallizations.

The French monarchists built their entire doctrine on the belief that the tradition of France was fundamentally aristocratic and monarchical, an idea conceivable only by people entirely hypnotized by the image of the France of Carlo Magno. René Johannet, a reactionary of a different breed, maintains that the tradition of France is absolutely bourgeois and that the nobility, in whom Maurras and his friends place their recalcitrant hope, has discarded as a ruling class since it had to become part of the gentry to survive. However, the social foundation of France is its peasant families, its laborious craftsmanship. The role of the dispossessed in the culmination of the bourgeois revolution has been ascertained. Thus, if the praxis of French socialism penetrated the nationalist declamation, the proletariat of France could also reveal to its country, without too much fatigue, a vast working-class tradition.

What this reveals to us is that tradition appears particularly invoked, and even fictitiously monopolized, by those least able to recreate it—of which no one should be surprised. The *pasadista* always has the paradoxical destiny of having a far more inferior understanding of the past than the futurist. The revolutionary has the faculty of thinking about history and the faculty of making or creating it. They may, perhaps, see a somewhat subjective image of the past, but it is animated and living. In contrast, the *pasadista* is incapable of representing it in his restlessness and capacity. Those who cannot imagine the future cannot, in general, imagine the past.

There is therefore no real conflict between the revolutionary and tradition, except for those who conceive tradition as a museum or a mummy. The only real conflict is with traditionalism. Revolutionaries embody the will of society not to petrify itself in a stadium, not to immobilize itself in an attitude. Sometimes society, paralyzed by a feeling of exhaustion or disenchantment, loses this creative will. But then its aging and decay will be inexorably confirmed.

The traditions of this epoch are being made by those iconoclasts who seem to deny all tradition. They are the active part of tradition. Without them, society would assume that tradition has lost its vitality and the ability to constantly renew and overcome itself.

Maurice Barrés bequeathed to his disciples a somewhat funereal definition of the Homeland. "The Homeland is the land and the dead." Barrés was himself a man with a funereal and morbid air, who according to Valle Inclán physically resembled a wet crow. But post-war generations are faced with the dilemma of burying with the spoils of Barrés, his thought of the solitary "paysan" obsessed with the excessive worship of the soil and its deceased. If, instead of surviving on their own thoughts, they are nourished by the very blood and hope of Barrés, they must resign to being buried themselves. They face the same situation with regards to traditionalism.

Source: *Peruanicemos al Perú*

9

FREEDOM OF EDUCATION

1. Freedom of education. Here's another program or perhaps another formula that has widespread consensus. But it is advisable to meditate more deeply on the practical value of this idea. The freedom of education seems, at first glance, the desired goal which all renovating efforts in a pedagogical sense must tend towards. But the ideology of the men who set out to transform our America cannot feed on fictions. The abstract value of an idea has no historical significance. What matters is its concrete value—especially for our America which is in great need of concrete ideals.

Concerning the current significance of the "freedom of education," we are not without instructive facts. One of the most considerable is undoubtedly the enthusiastic adherence to upholding this principle by Catholic politicians in Italy and France. The Italian Popular Party (PPI) has supported freedom of education as the most substantive of its demands. The Roman Catholic Church, shrewd and flexible in movements, presents itself as one of the greatest champions in the fight for the "freedom of education." It opposes the schooling of the secular world with the free school. Did it happen, perhaps, that in the decline of liberalism, the Roman church, traditional defender of authority and hierarchy, became liberal in turn? Let's not dwell on such subtle inquiries. The Church's policy towards the bourgeois-liberal state was defined many years ago in Veuillot's famous response to the evil liberal who was amazed that a Catholic of orthodox and rigid lineage became a vector of heretical freedom: "The liberty which you demand from us in the name of your principles, we deny you in the name of ours." In complete agreement with Veuillot, Roman Catholics of this time do not demand the freedom of education except where they are locked in the fight against secularism. Where teaching is not secular but Catholic, the Church categorically declares it to be freedom of education.

Naturally, this fact does not in itself devalue the "freedom of education." But it helps us to understand the relative and conventional aspects of this formula, in whose defense the hieratic custodians of tradition and several errant utopian gentlemen come together in various ways. Let's see the fruits of the labor of these renovators.

2. France offers us an interesting case in this regard. Who does not know something about the movement of *Les Compagnons de l'Université Nouvelle* (The Companions of the New University)? This movement was born in the trenches. It was a phenomenon of demobilization. Many combative university students and teachers, shaken by the excitement and victory of war, returned from the front, encouraged by a vigorous desire for renewal. They felt destined to build the New University. It was in the *compagnons* of old France, in the workers of the cathedrals of the Middle Ages, to whom they looked to for inspiration and as a model. The New University established the edifice of all teaching and of the entire school in its spirit and intention. The *Compagnons* intended to completely reorganize public education, and completely remake French democracy within the walls of the classroom. The war had made them heroic and strong. The war had given them a fighting will and revolutionary fervor. "It is necessary," they wrote:

> to rebuild the house from the foundations to the roof. Do not make illusions for yourselves, teachers. It is necessary to innovate everything, unite and cement everything. It is necessary to redo ideas, programs, methods and recruitment. It is more helpful to oppose the force of inertia, more helpful to organize our reform than to impose your experience on us. Your experience is your tradition and your tradition died with the Great War. Let's be clear. It is not the professors of 1900 who will make the France of 1950.

How is this reform carried out? "The new doctrine," the companions replied, "needs a new institution. Between the omnipotent and centralizing State, indifferent to inner lives, and the impotent, isolated, bitter citizens, it is necessary to introduce a middle ground: association, union organization. It is neces-

sary to introduce, between the State and the individual, the Union of Teachers for all educational levels—
primary, secondary, higher, professional—and in
each region. Alongside a political parliament, which is
an anachronism, and a revolutionary unionism, which
is unknown, we want to create new powers. We do not
want that past nor a violent future. We do not want life
to be fixed on political formulas, nor to precipitate instinctive triggers. We want it to be organized into a
corporation."

This program of the *Compagnons*, while proclaim-
ing the flaw of the Parliament and advocating the reorganization of education on the basis of a union, was
far from being a revolutionary program. Several European politicians arrived, effortlessly, to the analo-
gous disqualification of Parliament. For example,
Walter Rathenaú, in his scheme of the new state,
raised the need to create the educating state as a different body from the economic state and the political
state. The "companions" of the New University
seemed to find everything wrong in teaching, but only
in teaching. Overall, their awareness of France's problems was too corporate. Educated in the school of
democracy, they kept all their superstitions. "We
want a democratic education. Ours was not really
democratic, even if it tried very hard to appear so."
This is how these reformers wrote, evidently full of
good and healthy intentions, but no less obviously
naive as to the means of translating them into acts.
They did not figure out how to act out their program
once the teachers union was organized. They were
pleased to make this observation:

The State has failed in its efforts to centralize everything, not asking of the individual but his obedience and submission. Its immense management company has exceeded its strengths and capabilities, but has not given up on its claims. That is why today, instead of acting as a stimulant, it is often an obstacle and the interests for which it has been in charge languish. This is a general phenomenon.

Did the *Compagnons* believe that the State would voluntarily hand over power to the union? Did they believe that the State, out of love for pure democracy, would end up placing in its hands the power to reform education?

History, in any case, took a different course. Politicians of the national bloc, drunk with chauvinism and authoritarianism, were given power in the 1919 elections. Unfortunately, these same politicians did not completely take into account the generous plans of the faculty of the New University, branded *a priori* by their concomitance with the ideas of men like Edouard Herriot and Ferdinand Buisson.[1] Without consulting the friendly *Compagnons*, León Bérard[2] reformed secondary education not in the democratic sense that they advocated, but in a conservative sense, consistent with the tastes of the variety of species of reactionary and aristocratic thought. The National Bloc (BN) was already preparing to reform primary education when the voters, tired of their domination, decided to throw them out of the government. However, last year's elections (1924) did not inaugurate the democratic era envisioned by the *Compagnons*. These elections elevated Herriot—an eminent student teacher, friend of the New University, and supporter of the unique school—to the presidency. But they put him in front of too many urgent problems. And Herriot was unable to spend much time teaching.

Reviewing the battle of the *Compagnons,* C. Freinet recently wrote in a French magazine the following: "The Companions of the New University were not a force, that is, they were not capable of imposing their point of view. And this was because they were not able to organize the unity of the body of teachers. They had established, in all its details, the plan of the future cathedral. But they lacked the *compagnons* who were to build stone on stone. And it could not be otherwise because it was in the name of dying principles that they called workers to action."

3. In Germany, the revolution created a favorable situation for educational reform. It invited teachers and pedagogues—in whom a new consciousness had matured before the war, especially regarding elementary and secondary education—to try out their boldest ideas. The revolution had brought down the old regime. On its ruins, it was going to raise a new structure. In teaching, as in all fields, there could be complete renewal. The Weimar Constitution was inspired by the mentality and ideology of the most outspoken reformers of the German school. It established state-funded, compulsory public education until the age of 18. It proclaimed the right of the most capable to receive a post-secondary and university education. It declared the principle of freedom of education.

But even in theory this principle was not fully accepted in Weimar. The new German constitution carefully marked its boundaries. A commentator of this chapter of Weimar legislation specifies this particular limitation:

> In reality, what the Constitution assures in the declaration of Article 142, is that the State will ensure that every citizen and every child is guaranteed the education it creates, which agrees with their philosophical concepts and with their religion or that the parents consider necessary, and also, because the teachers educate according to their science and conscience, without breaking those same particular concepts. But this also has a limit, since the constitution orders that in all schools efforts tend to develop, within the spirit of German nationality and the reconciliation of peoples, moral education, civic sentiments, and personal and professional courage. That is to say, that there are philosophical concepts whose teaching does not fit within the constitution, which sets specific purposes for it, and the ends set by this provision coerce the freedom of education in a great way.[3]

On the other hand, it is interesting to note that the greatest innovations of the German educational reform have been those carried out in primary and secondary education. In this sector the will to renew has found many collaborators.

And reform has progressed in Saxony, Thuringia, and Hamburg. In other words, in the states where the political influence of the Socialists and Communists has prevailed.

Within the University, the spirit of the old regime

has persisted. A brave and energetic minority of teachers and students has tried to replace it with the New German spirit, but the University has remained the citadel of reaction. The University and the Republic have failed to understand each other. And there was no lack of those who declared a temporary closure of the State's Universities essential for the health of the republican regime. All this despite the principle of freedom of education having been sanctioned by the government.

4. The freedom of education is therefore nothing but a fiction. It is a utopia that history evicts. The State, whatever it is, cannot renounce the direction and control of public education. Why? For the notorious reason that the State is the organ of the ruling class. It has, therefore, the function of conforming teaching with the needs of this social class.

The State school educates contemporary youth in the principles of the bourgeoisie. Religious denominations have adapted their teaching to the same principles. In all conflicts between the interests of the ruling class and the method or ideas of public education, the State intervenes to restore the balance in favor of the former. Only in the periods in which the ends of the State and the School are intimately and regularly agreed upon, is the illusion of autonomy, spiritually and intellectually at least, of education possible.

The vanguard of Latin America should not fall in love with facades. They must sink their gaze within the depths of reality. Vain is all mental effort to conceive the apolitical school or the neutral school. The school of bourgeois order will continue to be a bourgeois school. The new school will come with the new order. The most reliable proof of this truth is offered by our time. The crisis of education universally coincides with a political crisis.

Source: *Temas de Educación*

10

PESSIMISM OF REALITY, OPTIMISM OF THE IDEAL

I

It seems to me that José Vasconcelos[1] has found a formula on pessimism and optimism that not only defines the feeling of the new Ibero-American generation in the face of the contemporary crisis, but also corresponds absolutely to the mentality and sensitivity of an era in which, despite Don José Ortega y Gasset's thesis on the "disenchanted soul" and "the twilight of revolutions," millions of men work with mystical courage and a religious passion to create a new world. "Pessimism of reality, optimism of the ideal," this is Vasconcelos' formula.

"Never settle, but always be above and beyond the moment," writes Vasconcelos. "Reject reality and struggle to destroy it, but not because of the absence of faith, but because of faith in human abilities and firm conviction that evil is never permanent or justifiable, and that it is always possible and feasible to redeem, purify, improve the collective state and private conscience."

The attitude of people who intend to correct reality is certainly more optimistic than pessimistic. They are pessimistic in their protest and in their condemnation of the present; but they are optimistic in their hope for the future. All great human ideals have started from a denial, but all have also been an affirmation. Religions have perennially represented in history that pessimism of reality and that optimism of the ideal that the Mexican writer is now preaching to us.

Those of us who are not content with mediocrity, those who are less satisfied with injustice, are often designated as pessimistic. But, in truth, pessimism dominates our spirit much less than optimism. We do not believe that the world should be fatally and eternally as it is. We believe that it can and should be better. The optimism we reject is the easy and lazy Panglossian optimism of those who think we live in the best of all possible worlds.

II

There are two kinds of pessimists as there are two kinds of optimists. Exclusively negative pessimism is limited to confirming with a gesture of helplessness and hopelessness, the misery of things and the vanity of efforts. He is a nihilist who waits, melancholy, for his last disappointment. But this kind of man is fortunately not common. It belongs to a rare hierarchy of disenchanted intellectuals. It is also a product of a time of decline or a people in collapse.

Among intellectuals, it is not uncommon that a simulated nihilism serves as a philosophical pretext to avoid their cooperation with any major renovation effort or to explain their disdain for any mass work. But the fictional nihilism of this type of intellectual is not even a philosophical attitude. It is reduced to a hidden and artificial disdain for great human myths. It is an unacknowledged nihilism that does not dare to appear on the surface of the work or the life of the negative intellectual who gives himself to this theoretical exercise as a solitary vice. The intellectual, nihilistic in private, is usually in public a member of an temperance league or an animal protection society. Their nihilism is only intended to guard and protect themselves from great passions. In the face of petty ideals, the false nihilist behaves with the most vulgar idealism.

III

It is with the pessimistic and negative spirits of this lineage that our optimism of the ideal refuses to let us be confused. Purely negative attitudes are sterile. Action is made of denials and affirmations. The new generation in our America, as in the whole world, is, above all, a generation that shouts its faith, that sings its hope.

IV

In contemporary Western philosophy a skeptical mood prevails. This philosophical attitude, as its critics emphasize, is a peculiar gesture of a civilization in decline. Only in a decadent world does a disenchanted feeling of life emerge. But even this contemporary skepticism or relativism has no relation, no affinity with the cheap and fictitious nihilism of the impotent, nor with the absolute and morbid nihilism of the suicidal madmen of Andreiev and Artzibachev. Pragmatism, which so effectively moves man to action, is basically a relativistic and skeptical school. Hans Vainhingher, the author of *Philosophie der Als Ob*, has been classified as a pragmatist. For this German philosopher there are no absolute truths, but there are relative truths that govern the life of man as if they were absolute. "Moral principles, just like aesthetic ones, legal criteria, just like those upon which science operates, the very foundations of logic, have no objective existence. They are fictitious constructions that serve only as regulatory precepts for our actions, which are conducted as if they were true."[2] Thus Giuseppe Renssi defines Vainhingher's philosophy, in his *Lineamentos de Filosofia esceptica*, which, as I see in a bibliographical note of Ortega y Gasset's magazine, has begun to attract interest in Spain and therefore in Spanish America.

This philosophy, therefore, does not call us to abandon action. It aims only to deny the Absolute. But it recognizes, in human history, the relative truth, the temporal myth of each age, the same value and the same efficacy as an absolute and eternal truth. This philosophy proclaims and confirms the need for myth and the usefulness of faith. Although then he entertains himself in thinking that all truths and all fictions, in the last analysis, are equivalent. Einstein, a relativist, behaves in life as an optimist of the ideal.

V

In the new generation, the desire to overcome skeptical philosophy burns. In the contemporary chaos, the materials of a new mysticism are being elaborated. The world in birth will not put its hope where the conceited religions put it. "The strong insist and fight," says Vasconcelos, "in order to anticipate somewhat the work of heaven." The new generation wants to be strong.

Source: *El Alma Matinal y Otras Estaciones del Hombre de Hoy*

NOTES

Introduction

1. Mariátegui, José Carlos. "The New Peru," and "The Problem of the Indian."

2. Vanden, Harry E. *National Marxism in Latin America: José Carlos Mariátegui's Thought and Politics* (1986).

3. *Ibid.*

4. Chavarria, Jesús. *José Carlos Mariátegui and the Rise of Modern Peru, 1890-1930* (1979). p. 75.

5. *Ibid*, p. 95.

6. Wise, David O. "Mariátegui's 'Amauta' (1926-1930), A Source of Peruvian Cultural History." *Revista Interamericana De Bibliografia* (1979), 29(3-4).

7. Del Prado, Jorge. "Mariátegui: Marxista-Leninista." *Dialéctica: Revista Continental de Teoría y Estudios Marxistas* (1943), 8(3), Havana, 38-56.

8. Vanden (1986), p. 123.

9. Del Prado (1943)

10. *Ibid.*

11. Becker, Marc. *Mariátegui and Latin American Marxist Theory* (1993).

12. Angotti, Tom. "The Contributions of José Carlos Mariátegui to Revolutionary Theory." *Latin American Perspectives* (1986), 13(33).

13. Mariátegui, "Marxist Determinism." p. 28 in this volume.

14. Becker (1993).

15. Liss, Sheldon B. *Roots of Revolution: Radical Thought in Cuba* (1987).

16. Pesce co-authored "The Problem of Race in Latin America" and presented it at the First Latin American Communist Conference in Buenos Aires in 1929.

17. Mariátegui. "The Heroic and Creative Sense of Socialism" in *José Carlos Mariátegui: An Anthology* (2011). Edited and translated by Harry E. Vanden and Marc Becker. p. 212.

18. Guevara, Ernesto. "Socialism and Man in Cuba." In *Che Guevara Reader: Writings on Politics and Revolution* (2003). p. 217.

19. Becker (1993).

20. Gutiérrez, Gustavo. *A Theology of Liberation* (1988).

21. Lenin, V.I. *State and Revolution* (2012), p. 7.

22. *José Carlos Mariátegui: an Anthology* (2011). Monthly Review Press.

23. *José Carlos Mariátegui, Seven Interpretive Essays on Peruvian Reality* (1971). University of Texas: Austin.

1. The World Crisis and the Peruvian Proletariat

1. José Ingenieros was an Argentinian socialist intellectual and university professor.

2. Adalberto Fonkén was anarcho-syndicalist labor leader.

3. This is likely a reference to *Freikorps* and *Reichswehr* suppression of the Ruhr Uprising which attempted to establish an independent socialist republic.

2. Marxist Determinism

1. The author is using this term in the sense of deriving truth from logic rather than practice.

2. de Man, Henri. *Au dela du Marxisme* (1929).

3. *Ibid.*

4. A far-right French political organization often considered the first fascist party.

5. *La Crisi Mondiale e Saggi critice di Marxismo e Socialismo* (1921).

3. The Problem of the Indian

1. *Gamonalismo/Gamonal*: Peruvian term for the latifundia system of landownership and relations of production; landowner or boss of a latifundia.

2. Due to the length of this note from the author, it has been placed at the end of the chapter.

3. Latifundia: Large landed estate owned by a wealthy landowner and worked by slaves and indentured servants.

4. *Encomienda/Encomendero*: Land granted to settlers in order to put an area under Spanish control, make it productive, and Christianize the Indigenous population; landowners are given control over local Indigenous people in return for acting in the political and economic interests of the Spanish crown.

5. Prada, González. "Nuestros Indios," in *Horas de Lucha*, 2nd ed.

6. Prada, *Horas de lucha*.

7. Bartolomé de las Casas (1484-1566) was a Spanish priest, bishop, and social reformer known for his part in revealing atrocities committed by the Spanish against Indigenous people. He was the first person to be given the title of *Protector de Indios* ("Protector of the Indians") which entailed advising the King of Spain on issues relating to Indigenous populations and speaking on behalf of the latter in legal matters.

4. The Problem of Race in Latin America

1. Pareto, Vilfredo. *The Mind and Society: A Treatise on General Sociology* (1935), pp. 626-27.

2. This region is know as the Sierra, which is considered one of Peru's three natural regions

along with the coast and montaña.

3. Bukharin, Nikolai. *Historical Materialism: A System of Sociology* (1925), pp. 127-128.

4. See Mariátegui's "The Problem of the Indian" in this volume.

5. A person with mixed Indigenous and European heritage.

6. This is a reference to *ayllu*, a traditional Andean community based on networks of families. This form of social organization predates the Incan Empire and is still in existence.

7. See Mariátegui, "The Problem of Land" in *Seven Interpretive Essays on Peruvian Reality* (1971).

8. Periods of forced labor of Indigenous peoples under Spanish colonizers.

9. A system of indentured servitude through debt peonage.

10. Guillermo Billinghurst (1851-1915) was the 31st President of Peru and member of the Civilista Party. Due to his administration's social reforms, he was overthrown by a military coup in 1914. The Department of Puno is located in southeast Peru and has a large population the Aymara Indians.

11. Queche term for the Incan Empire.

12. Published in *Amauta* No. 6.

13. *Yanaconazgo/Yanacona*: a feudalistic sharecropping system; tenant farmer or worker

14. This section was written primarily by Dr. Hugo Pesce using an outline provided by Mariátegui.

6. Ant-Imperialist Point of View

1. *Alianza Popular Revolucionaria Americana*, or American Popular Revolutionary Alliance, is a social-democratic party. In contrast to the Socialist Party, which would later be renamed the Communist Party, APRA appealed primarily to the urban middle class.

2. A working-class woman who tries to come off as belonging to the upper class or to actually become part of it.

7. Nationalism and Vanguardism

1. This term refers to adherents of a literary tradition that looks back on a romanticized Spanish past.

8. Heterodoxy of Tradition

1. Mariátegui, *El artista y la época*, p.129.

9. Freedom of Education

1. Herriot was a member of the Radical Party and three-time Prime Minister during France's Third Republic. Buisson was a French academic and left liberal politician who served as the head of the League of Education (1902-1906) and the Human Rights League (1914-1926).

2. Minister of Public Instruction (1919, 1921-1924), Vichy France ambassador to the Holy See (1940-1945).

3. Author unknown, *School Reform in Germany*. Contemporary Education Series.

10. Pessimism of Reality, Optimism of the Ideal

1. Vasconcelos was a Mexican writer, philosopher, and secretary of public education.

2. Guiseppi Rensi, *Lineamentos de Filosofia Escpetica*, 2nd Ed. (Bologna: Nicola Zanichelli, 1922).

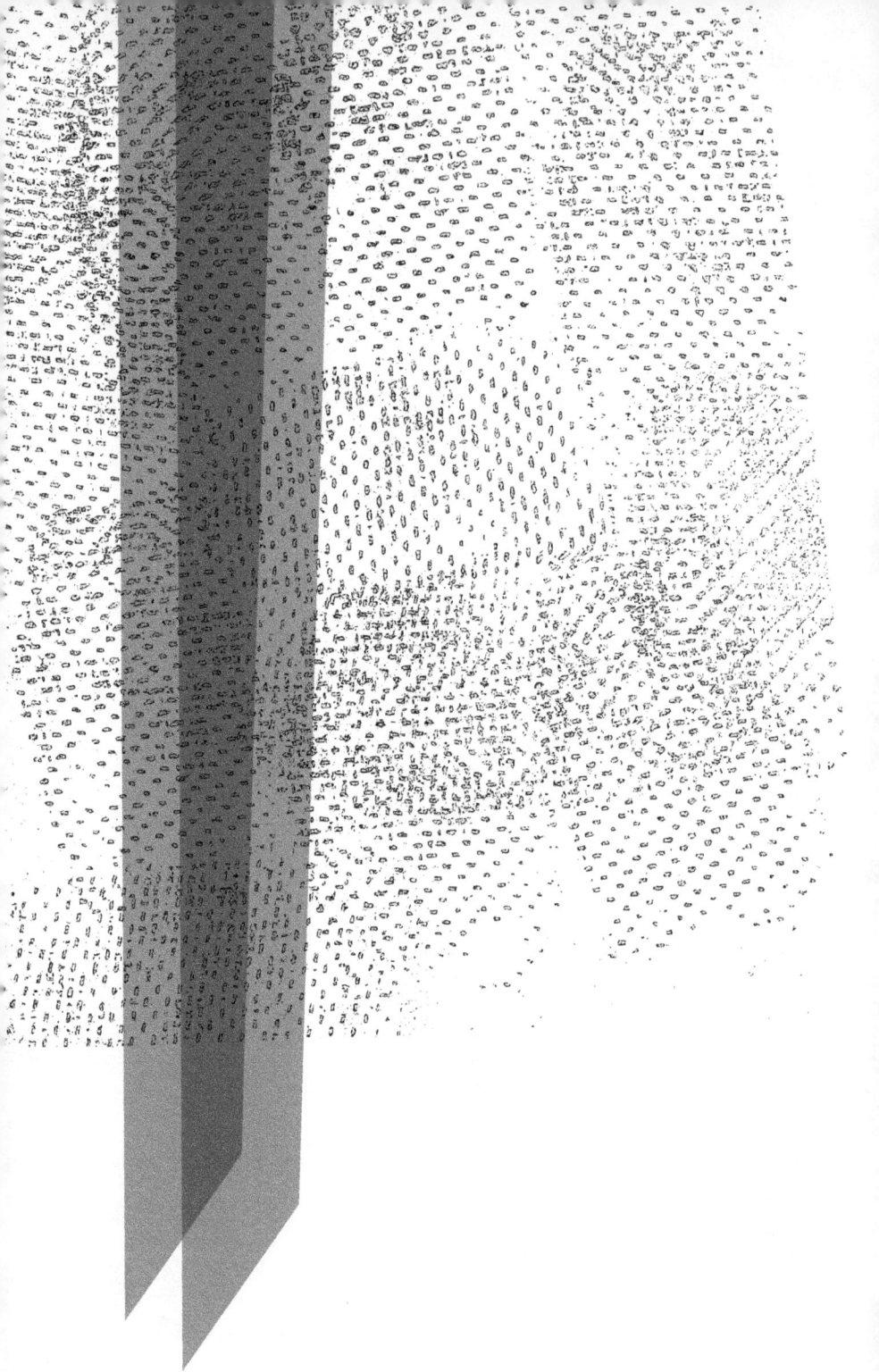

GLOSSARY

APRA: Alianza Popular Revolucionaria Americana, or American Popular Revolutionary Alliance, is a social-democratic party. Initially conceived as a Pan-American alliance, it was transformed into a Peruvian party centered on the country's urban middle class and gradual reformism.

*Ayllu***:** A traditional Andean community based on networks of families. This communal form of social organization and production predates the Incan Empire and is still in existence today.

*Encomienda/Encomendero***:** Land granted to settlers in order to put an area under Spanish control, make it productive, and Christianize the Indigenous population; Landowners given control over local Indigenous people in return for acting in the political and economic interests of the Spanish crown.

Enganche: Forced indentured servitude through debt peonage.

Gamonalismo/Gamonal: Peruvian term for the latifundia system of landownership and relations of production; landowner or boss of a latifundia.

Hacienda: Large estate or plantation.

Latifundia: Large estate owned by a wealthy landowner and worked by slaves and indentured servants.

Mita: Periods of forced labor of Indigenous peoples under Spanish colonizers.

Pasadismo: A literary tradition that looks back on a romanticized Spanish past.

Peruvian Socialist Party (PSP)/Peruvian Communist Party (PCP): a Marxist-Leninist vanguard party founded in 1928 with Mariátegui serving as the first secretary-general. In contrast to the petit-bourgeois reformism of APRA, it sought to unite the country's urban and rural working class under the direction of a core group of communists and connect the national struggle to the internationalist communist movement via the Third International. It was renamed the Peruvian Communist Party shortly after Mariátegui's death in 1930.

***Yanaconazgo/Yanacona*:** A feudalistic sharecropping system; tenant farmer or worker.

BIBLIOGRAPHY

Angotti, Tom (1986). "The Contributions of José Carlos Mariátegui to Revolutionary Theory." in *Latin American Perspectives*, 13(33), 33-57.

Becker, Marc (1993). Mariátegui *and Latin American Marxist Theory*. Latin American Series, No. 20. Center for International Studies: Athens.

Chavarria, Jesús (1979). *José Carlos Mariátegui and the Rise of Modern Peru, 1890-1930*. University of New Mexico: Albuquerque.

Del Prado, Jorge (1943), "Mariátegui: Marxista-Leninista" in *Dialéctica: Revista Continental de Teoría y Estudios Marxistas*, 8(3), Havana, 38-56.

Guevara, Ernesto (2003). *Che Guevara Reader: Writings on Politics and Revolution*. Ocean Press.

Gutiérrez, Gustavo (1988). *A Theology of Liberation*. Orbis Books: New York.

Lenin, Vladimir (2012). *State and Revolution*. International Publishers: New York.

Liss, Sheldon B. (1987). *Roots of Revolution: Radical Thought in Cuba*. University of Nebraska: Lincoln.

Mariátegui, José Carlos (1971). *Seven Interpretive Essays on Peruvian Reality*. Trans. Marjory Urquidi. University of Texas: Austin.

— (2011). *José Carlos Mariátegui: an Anthology*. Ed. Harry E. Vanden and Marc Becker. Monthly Review Press: New York.

Vanden, Harry E. (1986). *National Marxism in Latin America: José Carlos Mariátegui's Though and Politics*.

Wise, David O. (1979). "Mariátegui's 'Amauta' (1926-1930), A Source of Peruvian Cultural History." *Revista Interamericana   de Bibliografia*, 29(3-4).